US 9th Air Force
Bases in Essex
1943–44

AVIATION
HERITAGE TRAIL SERIES

US 9th Air Force Bases in Essex 1943–44

Martin W. Bowman

Pen & Sword
AVIATION

First published in Great Britain in 2010 by
PEN & SWORD AVIATION
an imprint of
Pen & Sword Books Ltd
47 Church Street
Barnsley
South Yorkshire
S70 2AS

ISBN: 978 1 84884 332 5

A CIP catalogue record for this book is available from
the British Library

Typeset in Times New Roman by S L Menzies-Earl

Printed in the UK by CPI UK

Pen & Sword Books Ltd incorporates the imprints of:
Pen & Sword Aviation, Pen & Sword Maritime, Pen & Sword
Military, Wharncliffe Local History, Pen & Sword Select, Pen &
Sword Military Classics, Leo Cooper, Remember When,
Seaforth Publishing and Frontline Publishing.

For a complete list of Pen & Sword titles please contact:
Pen & Sword Books Limited
47 Church Street, Barnsley, South Yorkshire, S70 2AS, England
E-mail: enquiries@pen-and-sword.co.uk
Website: www.pen-and-sword.co.uk

CONTENTS

ACKNOWLEDGEMENTS

Essex County Council Tourism; Graham Simons at GMS Enterprises; the 2nd Air Division Memorial Library, Norwich; Nigel McTeer; Roy West; Paul Wilson.

PROLOGUE

This is a story about the Marauders and the kids who fly and fight in them. The Marauder has had some rough going over here in the Big League. A lot of people had to be sold on it. Arthur Brisbane once said: 'God thought up the best advertisement – the rainbow. And he was smart enough to reserve the best space for it.'

Air power over here in Britain has sold itself in the same space. Day after day and night after night, you hear the roar of bombers and fighters over London, reminding all the men who make decisions in high places that no city is safe from air power. Great advertising.

Air power has sold itself by performance. That's the only way an individual plane, like the Marauder, can sell itself. The Marauder should have had a head start – the name of the maker has been a byword that dates back nearly to Kittyhawk. But it ran into sales resistance none the less.

The bombers Glenn Martin makes are the heroes of this story. The B-26 Martin Marauder, medium bomber, came to this front several months ago. They used them first on low-level stuff. The first job was a sweet one; no losses. Twelve of them hit a power station in Holland early in May. Then they went out once more to hit another target in Holland. But this time they got the hell knocked out of them. They just got shot down. That was all. Period. And it was period, too, for the Marauders.

There were a couple of rough jokes being told on Fortress stations about the plane: 'Have you heard about the wire they sent to the Martin plant? You've got a fine plane, but we suggest one modification: Put four silver handles on it like a proper coffin should have.'

Another one was aimed at the Marauder's lack of wing span. They called them the Baltimore vagrants – no visible means of support. And the most cutting crack of all was this one: 'The Marauder is a beautiful piece of machinery, but it will never take the place of the airplane.'

They had just about buried the Marauders when a stubborn guy named Thatcher, from Maryland, came over with a new group.

They tell me he flew the first B-26 off the line. He was convinced the Marauder was a good plane for this theatre, and his was the group that first proved it.

Tactics were shifted; instead of hedge-hopping, they went out at medium altitudes, and bombed in formation like their big-brother Forts. Spits covered their raids, as they had covered the first of the Fortress jobs. The Marauders flew 4,000 sorties – that means that a total of 4,000 planes went out on a total of 75 raids between the end of May and the end of September. The total loss was only 13 – only one shot down by fighters, the rest bagged by flak. The 'Ugly Duckling' had lost its label.

Main target of the Marauders was the Nazi airfields in France, the fields from which Nazi fighter planes would fly to stop an invasion. The Marauder tactics were dress rehearsal for the Big Push.

Captain John R. 'Tex' McCrary

When the 322nd Bomb Group (Medium) commanded by Lieutenant Colonel Robert M. 'Moose' Stillman arrived at Bury St Edmunds (Rougham) in March 1943 it had been decided to employ the Martin B-26 Marauder in low-level attacks against industrial targets in France and the Low Countries. The 322nd Bomb Group trained in low-level operations for eight weeks and flew its first combat mission on 14 May. In four hours VIIIth Bomber Command attacked four targets, losing twelve B-17s and B-24s and claiming sixty-seven fighters shot down. The Marauders returned safely from their target, the PEN electricity-generating plant at Velsen near Ijmuiden on the Dutch coast, but when Stillman was called to a conference at HQ, Elveden Hall near Thetford he was informed that reconnaissance photos of the plant had revealed no damage and was still in full operation. Stillman was informed that VIIIth Bomber Command wanted the target to be attacked again on 17 May. Stillman could not believe it and stated that to attack the same target so soon could mean enemy defences would be ready and waiting for them. General Newton L. Longfellow, VIIIth Bomber Command, was adamant that the attack should go ahead and although he sympathised with Colonel Stillman's point of view, Longfellow threatened Stillman with the loss of his command if he refused to obey orders. Upset at the thought of sending his crews back to the same target so soon after their harrowing first mission (where they suffered a number of casualties and lost Lieutenant Howell and his crew in a crash near the base), Stillman returned to Rougham near Bury St Edmunds. The order for the mission arrived at 0036 hours on 17 May asking for a maximum effort raid, flying the same route as three days before. Lieutenant Colonel Alfred Von Kolnitz, the 322nd Bomb Group's Chief Intelligence Officer, was alarmed that the same route was to be flown, as he expected heavy enemy opposition. He wrote a memo to Colonel Stillman, ending it: 'For God's sake, get fighter cover!'

The crews alerted for the mission were from the 450th and 452nd Squadrons, who with four exceptions had not flown the first mission. One of these was Colonel Stillman, who was determined to lead. The 322nd could field eleven B-26 Marauders for the mission, with aircraft of the 452nd Squadron leading. Although the crews were confident of a second success, they all expected to meet stiff opposition and many were convinced they would not return. Stillman was also convinced that the mission was going to be a disaster, but was determined to do his duty and ensure the target was knocked out this time.

As he left the Intelligence Section after the mission briefing, Lieutenant Colonel Von Kolnitz said, 'Cheerio.'

Stillman answered, 'No, it's goodbye.'

Trying to cheer him up, Von Kolnitz said, 'I'll see you at one o'clock.'

'It's goodbye,' replied Stillman firmly. At 1050 hours the Marauders began taking off. At 1147 hours and thirty-three miles off the coast of Holland Captain Stephens in the 452nd flight aborted due to power failure to the top turret and one engine not giving the correct boost. Off course, the remaining B-26s crossed the Dutch coast twenty-five miles from Noordwijk and headed toward Rozenburg Island in the Maas River Estuary, the most heavily defended area in the Netherlands. They were showered by 20-mm cannon shells. The lead aircraft took direct hits, which severed the flight controls and killed Lieutenant Resweber, Stillman's co-pilot. As a result of the loss of flying controls the Marauder snap rolled and Stillman saw the ground coming up to meet him. His plane crashed upside down, but amazingly, Stillman, Sergeant Freeman and Sergeant Willis were all pulled from the wreckage alive. The two sergeants survived the first mission and had now been lucky again.

The following flight, which was two miles to the south, also encountered heavy fire from the ground. Lieutenant Garrambone's aircraft was hit, he lost control and the aircraft crashed into the Maas

River. Garrambone and three of his crew survived. Believing that they were approaching the target area, pilots and navigators looked for the landmarks they had noted on the mission briefing. As they were way off course there were none and they were flying somewhere between Delft and Rotterdam. Captain Converse now led the first flight and taking evasive action to avoid flak collided with Lieutenant Wolf's aircraft, which was leading the second element. Both B-26s went down but four gunners survived from the two aircraft, one being Sergeant Thompson, the fourth veteran of 14 May. Debris hit *Chickersaw Chief* causing the pilot, Lieutenant Wurst, to crash-land the B-26 in a field near Meije. Sergeant Heski the top turret gunner lost a foot in the crash and he was the only serious casualty. This left only Lieutenant F. H. Matthews and Lieutenant E. R. Norton of the third element of the lead flight in the air. Norton's co-pilot was his twin brother, J. A. Norton. These two aircraft joined the second flight to make a more effective force to bomb the target. Unfortunately, the second flight was as lost as the first and had no idea where the target lay. Forty-five miles into Holland the remaining aircraft decided to turn for home. Lieutenant Colonel William Purinton, who was leading the second flight, asked his navigator, Lieutenant Jeffries, for a heading. Jeffries answered, '270°' followed by 'Hold it a minute, I think I see the target. Yes, there it is!' Bomb doors were opened and Purinton's co-pilot, Lieutenant Kinney sighted and dropped the bombs on what they thought was the target. (In reality it was the gasholder in the suburbs of Amsterdam.) All aircraft dropped their bombs when Kinney dropped his but they were heading directly towards the 'real' target at Ijmuiden. There they encountered more heavy flak and Purinton's plane was hit but he managed to ditch two miles offshore. Jeffries was killed in the crash and a German patrol boat picked up the rest of the crew. Lieutenant Jones' aircraft was the next to be shot down and crashed. Lieutenant Aliamo was the only survivor. The Norton brothers, now flying at 250 mph to try and make it home, were shot down west of Ijmuiden. Their tail gunner, Sergeant Longworth, was the only survivor of their crew.

Only Lieutenant Matthews and Captain Jack Crane now remained, at some distance apart. They survived the coastal flak and raced for England. When the Marauders crossed the coast on their inbound flight, twenty-six FW 190s of II./JG1 on a combat alert from Woensdrecht, southern Holland, were vectored to meet them. At 1218 hours they saw Matthews' and Crane's aircraft flying low and fast over the North Sea and they attacked. Crane said to the top turret gunner and engineer, Staff Sergeant George Williams, 'Come up front, George, there is something wrong with the rudder.' Williams checked the rudder cables and repaired a damaged section with some safety wire from the rear of the turret. As he returned to the turret the aircraft was peppered with bullets and he saw the port engine in flames. He called to Crane but there was no reply. The plane started to lose altitude, levelled off and then dived into the sea. (Williams and Sergeant Jesse Lewis, tail gunner, scrambled to safety out of the camera hatch, climbed into a life raft and watched the Marauder sink in about forty-five seconds. The time was 1224 hours and they were eighty miles from England. They spent five days in the raft before being rescued and returned to England and to the 322nd Bomb Group. Lieutenant Matthews' B-26 was shot into the sea at 1230 hours. There were no survivors. *Feldwebel* Niedereichholz of *Stab* II./JG1 and *Oberfeldwebel* Winkler of 4./JG3 were the victorious *Jagdflieger.*) At Rougham, the estimated time for the Group's return was 1250 hours. On the control tower balcony, General Brady of VIIIth Bomber Command and other watchers were growing apprehensive. At 1305 hours a RAF listening post reported that it had intercepted a German radio transmission, which said that it had shot two bombers into the sea. By 1330 hours it was decided that no aircraft were still airborne and that a disaster had occurred, with all ten B-26s being lost.

Of the sixty airmen shot down in enemy territory, twenty-two survived as PoWs. Whilst a prisoner in *Stalag Luft* III, Colonel Stillman surmised that the mission was a disaster and one factor had contributed to its failure. When Captain Stephens aborted at the start of the mission, he climbed to 1,000 feet. Stillman did not blame him for this, as it was standard operating procedure for the B-26 in order to allow the crew to bail out if necessary. However, Stillman was convinced that in so doing Stephens had unwittingly exposed his aircraft to enemy radar, thus alerting the Germans to the presence of the rest of the force. As a result of the disaster of 17 May, the 322nd Bomb Group was stood down and it was deemed suicidal to fly the Martin Marauder at low level, so tactics were rethought and the B-26 was used at medium level and from bases in Essex so that fighter cover for them could be improved.

On Sunday 13 June when 102 B-17s of the 1st Wing were assigned to Bremen while the 4th Wing went to Kiel for another raid on the U-boat yards, the 94th, 95th and 96th Bomb Groups took off from their bases at Earls Colne in Essex, Framlingham in Suffolk and Andrews

Field in Essex for the last time. On their return from the raid they touched down at the former B-26B/C Marauder bases at Bury St Edmunds (Rougham) and Horham in Suffolk and Snetterton Heath in Norfolk respectively and the 322nd, 323rd and 386th Medium Bomb Groups transferred to airfields in Essex, where they joined the 387th at Chipping Ongar. The 322nd Bomb Group moved to Andrews Field near Braintree to resume operations on 31 July 1943. Colonel Glen C. Nye, the man who had nursed the 322nd Bomb Group in the early days of its existence before Colonel Stillman, took command.

INTRODUCTION

By far the largest tactical air component in the European Theatre of Operations (ETO) was the 9th Air Force. Before the entry of the United States of America into the Second World War on 7 December 1941, a body known as V Air Support Command had been constituted. In April 1942 this new Command was redesignated as the US 9th Air Force and as such was sent to Egypt in the autumn of that year. The 9th Air Force began operations in November 1942 in support of the

Major General Samuel E. Anderson (left) commander of IX Bomber Command, being interviewed by Lowell Thomas. (*USAF*)

Major General Otto P. Weyland, commander of XIX Tactical Air Command. (USAF)

Allied drive across Egypt and Libya and took part in the fighting in Tunisia and the invasions of Sicily and mainland Italy. When the initial planning for an invasion of continental Europe began, it was realised that an essential constituent of the scheme would be a tactical air force. To provide this element, the 9th Air Force was effectively disbanded in the Middle East and was re-formed on 16 October 1943 at a headquarters at Bushey Hall, Watford, north-west of London, under the command of Brigadier General Samuel E. Anderson. The 9th Air Force were to take a major part in the war of attrition leading up to the invasion and to follow the invasion forces on a fully mobile basis toward the eventual conquest of Nazi Germany.

The new IX Bomber Command took over the 3rd Bombardment Wing from 8th Air Force Air Support Command and its four medium bomber groups in Essex – the 322nd at Andrews Field, the 323rd at Earls Colne, the 386th at Great Dunmow and the 387th at Chipping Ongar – were assigned. Three Fighter Groups began to arrive in November 1943 and by 8 December they had been placed under 70th Fighter Wing control in IX Fighter Command. Two of these Groups, the 357th at Raydon and the 362nd at Wormingford, flew P-47s, while the 354th Fighter Group at Boxted flew P-51 Mustangs. VIII Fighter Command badly needed a long-range escort fighter to escort the heavies but it was not until the 357th Fighter Group and its P-51Bs at Raydon was transferred to the 8th Air Force in exchange for the P-47-equipped 358th Fighter Group that the 8th Air Force had its long-range escort fighter. By 1944 fourteen P-47 groups, three P-51 groups and one P-38 fighter group were serving in the 9th Air Force.

After a report submitted on 10 April 1944 on the bombing errors of the 394th and 344th Bomb Groups Lieutenant General Brereton stated the bombing of these units showed 'lack of aggressiveness, improper tactics and techniques and a lack of training....' It was then decided to remove the groups from operations for one week where additional training seemed imperative. The 323rd Bomb Group, which had been operational since 15 July 1943, was the first to receive this training and was followed by other groups. Precision bombing was emphasised in the training and crews were encouraged to be alert in correcting errors and the source of errors. By the end of April these efforts began to bear fruit and the bombing of IX Bomber Command started to show marked improvement.

In May 1944 the 9th Air Force was powerfully equipped to support the D-Day invasion. Its mission was to gain and maintain air superiority; disrupt hostile lines of communication; to destroy enemy troops and materiel on the fighting front in cooperation with forward ground forces. Long-range, deep attacks on enemy production centres and large cities in the rear were not part of the tactical air job. The tactical air force was engaged directly against enemy personnel, materiel, transport, shelter and fortifications either in or on the way to the fighting zone. The speed with which the 9th Air Force frequently had to plan and execute operations, the variable strength of the operational unit (depending upon the size and vulnerability of the

Captain Darrell R. Lindley, 394th Bomb Group, who posthumously received the Medal of Honor for his actions on 9 August 1944. (USAF)

target) and the relatively short range, with multiple 'turn-around' missions, at which fighter-bombers were normally applied imposed a set of organisational necessities which were not encountered on a comparable scale by any other American air force.

The principal weapon was the fighter-bomber, armed with bombs, bullets and frequently with rockets and chemical fire bombs. Without its bombs it was a powerful, dangerous fighter, which outmatched the *Luftwaffe* in the air whenever they met. With bombs and machine guns it destroyed thousands of enemy aircraft and air installations on or near airfields as well as enemy road and rail lines and transport on the move. Backed by, a highly developed system of tactical radar control and excellent air-ground communications which permitted immediate reaction to developments in the air and on the ground, the fighter-bomber was the most effective aircraft of the war in close-in cooperation with ground elements and in the neutralisation or destruction of enemy personnel, materiel and installations in the immediate battle area.

The medium and light bombers, which, like the fighter-bombers, formed the largest single force of their type in the USAAF, were organised and employed quite differently. The bombers were not used in routine daily operations based on the tactical requirements of any particular army, nor were they assigned to or divided among the tactical air commands. Experience proved that they were employed efficiently in Phase 2 precision-bombing operations against static targets such as communications centres, bridges, and railway yards and against such objectives as supply depots and fuel and ammunition dumps. The relative importance of these targets could best be measured at air force level and their systematic destruction planned and executed only after a thorough appraisal of the tactical situation over the entire army group front, with a view to meeting most efficiently and effectively the total air force commitment. Medium and light bombardment was preserved as a single striking force which, however, was often divided to attack many targets simultaneously. The air force's medium of control of these aircraft was 9th Bombardment Division.

IX Air Defence Command, the first of its kind assigned to any US air force in World War 2, participated in counter-air force operations and was particularly successful in counter-V-bomb operations. It was equipped with signal air warning systems and with various types of air defence weapons, including a heavy proportion of anti-aircraft artillery.

The IX Engineer Command was created for effective operational control and administration of more than 20,000 aviation engineer personnel and was responsible for developing, constructing and rehabilitating air fields and installations. The seventh and largest major command was the IX Air Force Service Command with 60,000 officers and men. Because of the mobility and flexibility of the entire air force it was faced with many unusual problems, as well as the constant responsibility of maintaining supply and maintenance service along rapidly lengthening lines of communications over a ninety-mile stretch of sea and hundreds of miles of land. Among its many tasks were the assembly of aircraft such as P-51s and P-38s shipped over the Atlantic into British ports and the assembly of over 4,000 CG-4 gliders, each of which arrived in five large packing cases. The record for glider assembly was 100 in a single day. IX Air Force Service Command also set up a series of Tactical Air Depots, where aircraft of specific types were given major overhauls.

The pre-invasion activities of the 9th Air Force were marked by a very rapid physical growth, exceedingly intricate and detailed organisational planning and experiment and, during the latter months of the period, large-scale 'softening up' operations against continental installations to pave the way for invasion. During the first few months in the United Kingdom under the command of Lieutenant General Lewis H. Brereton the 9th Air Force concentrated on activating, organising, training and equipping the many specialised tactical, technical and service units which would be the major air component of the Allied invasion forces. The 9th Air Force from 16 October 1943 until D-Day grew from four to forty-five tactical groups, from fewer than 300 to more than 1,100 bombers, from none to more than 3,000 troop-carrier aircraft and gliders and from fewer than 50,000 to considerably more than 200,000 personnel. Long before D-Day it was apparent that flexibility and mobility was needed and the 9th Air Force had to pioneer its own tactical air cooperation and form its command and inter-command relationships and structure. This was based on the limited experience of the RAF and three groups of P-40s and two groups of B-25s of the 9th Air Force in the Middle East–Cyrenaica and Libya.

Although in late 1943 and the winter of 1943–44 the 9th Air Force emphasised build-up and planning, it simultaneously carried out medium bomber and long-range fighter operations, which formed a comparatively small but significant part of the air campaign from Britain. The first phase of these operations, which had been initiated by medium bombers before the reconstitution of the 9th Air Force in Britain, was a series of diversionary attacks on the belt of German coastal airfields in France, Belgium and Holland, which were used as bases for enemy fighters opposing the passage of 8th Air Force heavy bombers. Although the medium bomber force was small and although the necessity for contact flying both in target and base areas restricted the number of operational days, these counter-air force operations contributed materially to forcing the *Luftwaffe* to draw its fighters inland, where they represented a less serious threat not only to the 'heavies' but to the invasion forces which were to arrive in Normandy on 6 June 1944. The airfield targets and *Noball* or V-1 rocket bomb targets were the main preoccupation of the 9th's bomber force until February 1944, when the stress shifted to railway centres surrounding and connecting the possible invasion points. The flying bomb and the curious ski-shaped ramps in France were to be the launch sites for a new reign of terror against London and southern England. The *Vergelrungswaffe* I (Revenge Weapon No. 1) was a small, pilotless aircraft with a 1,870-lb HE warhead that detonated on impact. On 5 December 1943 the bombing of the *Noball* sites became part of the Operation *Crossbow* offensive. Photoreconnaissance aircraft regularly photographed each V-1 site before and after an attack and by the end of the month, the Allies had over-flown forty-two *Noball* sites, of which thirty-six were revealed as having been damaged, twenty-one of them seriously. By 12 June 1944 sixty weapons sites had been identified. Hitler's 'rocket blitz' began on 13 June when ten V-1s, or

'Doodlebugs' as they became known, were launched against London from sites in north-eastern France. The maximum bomb load for the Marauders was 4,000 lb and experience showed that 2 x 2,000-lb bombs were required when attacking bridges; for *Noball* targets they used 8 x 500-lb bombs as well as other combinations.

During the intensive campaign against the V-1 sites Marauder squadrons averaged one V-1 site destroyed for every 182 tons of bombs dropped, compared with 219 tons for Mitchells, 165.4 tons for B-17 Flying Fortresses and just 39.8 tons of bombs for Mosquitoes. By the end of September 1944, when the Allied advance overran most of the sites, 133 V-1 installations had been identified by photoreconnaissance aircraft. Only eight ever remained undiscovered by aerial reconnaissance. Air Chief Marshal Sir Trafford Leigh-Mallory cited in this statement: 'Of all the bomber forces involved, those of the 9th Air Force proved to be by far the most efficacious in knocking out these difficult and defended targets.'

By May 1944 the 9th Air Force had grown very nearly to full strength and dispatched an average of more than 1,000 aircraft daily against enemy lines of communication leading into and supporting the Atlantic wall defences, both in the Calais and the Normandy areas and against all types of enemy transport on rails, roads and rivers, to

Clearing snow off Marauders of the 387th Bomb Group and the runway at Clastres around Christmas 1944. The Group began their occupation of the airfield on 4 November 1944. (USAF)

Two 2,000-lb bombs fall from the bomb bays of two 344th Bomb Group Marauders on the Group's 200th combat mission in 1945. (*USAF*)

prevent supply, reinforcement and re-fortification of the vital sectors. As the invasion approached IX Bomber Command and the IX and XIX Tactical Air Commands were given full responsibility for a systematic programme of interdiction which called for the destruction of all major railway and highway bridges crossing the Seine from Paris to the English Channel, from Normandy and Brittany in the west and from Pas de Calais and the Low Countries' coast in the east. This programme was pursued until only one road bridge was serviceable between Conflans and Rouen and the enemy was forced to follow circuitous, slow, and costly routes to move troops and supplies to the beaches. At the same time the bombardment force began late in the spring to carry out difficult precision bombing attacks against the large anti-invasion guns in use or under construction on the French coast.

Reconnaissance, daily becoming increasingly important in the tactical sphere of operations, was fitted into the total air force operational scheme in order to provide vast quantities of detailed intelligence to the ground forces for the assault stage, as well as to furnish clues for most effective bomber and fighter-bomber employment. High reconnaissance, for instance, revealed extensive beach defence construction on the French shore, while low (10 to 50 feet true altitude), extremely hazardous 'dicing' missions undertaken by the Photo Reconnaissance Group accomplished possibly the war's most remarkable and valuable photography, by providing close-range, easily interpreted photographs of the intimate details of the beach defences along the full length of the potential invasion coast, including the Calais sector.

On D-Day major air assignments for IX Bomber Command were to attack three coastal batteries at first light, three more twenty to five minutes before H-Hour, and to attack seven defended localities in the *Utah* area. IX Bomber Command dispatched 1,011 aircraft, of which 823 made attacks. This averaged five-plus boxes (a compact formation of aircraft) per group and for the first time more aircraft were dispatched than there were crews available, and so many crews flew on two missions. Coastal batteries in the British area and on the north-west tip of the Cherbourg peninsula were attacked. Road junctions or highway bridges were visited in both the British and US areas and B-26s and A-20s attacked four marshalling yards east of the Seine in the afternoon. Take-off of IX Bomber Command aircraft was accomplished between 0343 and 0500 hours, but weather and pathfinder difficulties reduced the effectiveness of the attacks considerably. Of the first three batteries attacked only one B-26 was over the battery at Benerville and eleven were over the two batteries at Ouistreham. Results at the other three batteries were unobserved for one and good to excellent at two. Owing to weather conditions the attacks on the seven defended localities were made at extremely low altitude, from 3,500 to 7,000 feet. A total of 269 aircraft dropped 523.63 tons of 250-lb bombs. Results of all attacks were difficult to determine, but the ground commander in the *Utah* area stated the pinpoint bombing of the beach targets was excellent. The light resistance encountered by a 101st Airborne unit in occupying a battery west of St Martin de Varreville was assessed as 'due to the excellent air force bombing.'

By the end of the day the B-26s and A-20s had contributed over 1,000 sorties to the 4,656 flown by all elements of the 9th Air Force in support of the greatest invasion in history. The AAF official history said, 'Where the effects of part of the "mediums" effort on *Utah* Beach could be later followed, 35 per cent of the bombs were reported to have fallen to seaward of high water mark, but 43 per cent [were] within 300 feet of their target'. To quote Herman Goering: 'The Allies owe the success of the invasion to their air forces. They prepared the invasion; they made it possible; and they carried it through.' Medium and light bombers, taking off before dawn, carried out eleventh-hour attacks against powerful German defensive gun batteries on *Utah* Beach and later in the day switched to communications centres, command posts, supply depots and other targets in the enemy's immediate rear. The First US Army reported that enemy coastal defences were much less formidable than had been expected and it attributed much of this surprising weakness to the power of tactical air attacks on the shore before and during D-Day.

Flying approximately 2,300 sorties in twenty hours, fighter-bombers had the general commitments of protecting the cross-Channel movement, preparing the way for landings by neutralising beach defences, protecting troops actually on the beaches, reducing the enemy's ability to mount an effective counter-attack by denying him the use of roads into the battle area and, finally, providing cooperation in the advance of ground forces inland from the assault areas. Scores of reports from captured German commanders described the difficulty of travelling on all roads leading to the front in daylight, the necessity of using aircraft spotters on all vehicles and the failure of troops to reach their positions in the line at full strength, on time or in an orderly fashion. General Fritz Bayerlein, commander of the *Panzer Lehr* division, said that his unit took eighty hours to reach the front and arrived with only 50 per cent of its original firepower. Von Rundstedt complained too that the incessant fighter-bomber attacks on roads and rails, as well as the bomber attacks on larger communications centres, prevented the shifting of reserves which could have defeated the Allies on the beaches.

Apart from its strike aircraft, the 9th Air Force was the operator of the most formidable troop-carrying force ever assembled. On D-Day no fewer than fifty-six squadrons in fourteen troop-carrier groups were in action carrying paratroops or towing gliders. Almost all the aircraft were C-47 Skytrains and the gliders mainly Waco CG-4s, plus a number of British-built Horsas. Under the 9th Air Force the IX Troop Carrier Command organised, planned and successfully executed the greatest troop-carrier operation in history, the delivery of paratroops and airborne units behind the German lines on the Cherbourg Peninsula, and maintained resupply and medical evacuation operations

Bombing up Marauder B-26B 41-31755 with 1,000-pounders. *(USAF)*

for several months after D-Day. IX Troop Carrier Command was transferred to the First Allied Airborne Army about three months after D-Day.

The first units of IX Engineer Command landed on *Utah* Beach on D-Day and on *Omaha* Beach on D+1. An emergency landing strip was completed on *Utah* by 2115 hours on D-Day. The build-up of aviation engineer units proceeded approximately on schedule: by D+5 four battalions were ashore and construction was well under way on three fighter-bomber airfields on *Omaha* and one on *Utah*. By D+6 five fighter-bomber groups were based in Normandy and participated in the all-out air assault on the outer defences of Cherbourg. By 30 June (D+24) nine all-weather airfields had been completed on the continent and seven others were under construction. From 6 June to 24 July the 9th Air Force concentrated upon maintaining undiminished operations against the enemy in cooperation with ground forces and upon transferring tactical units to the continent as rapidly as possible. By 24 July thirteen fighter-bomber groups and one reconnaissance group had crossed the Channel and a highly efficient and effective radar control system had been established on the beachhead without losing a single day of operations. Continuing to operate from Britain, medium and

Hasselt, forty miles east of Brussels, a main line rail junction and depot between Antwerp and Germany, under attack by 200 Marauders on 10 April 1944. The white smoke shooting up is an ammunition train which left a crater 150 feet by 40 feet. All through traffic lines were cut, one of them in seventeen places, by 1,000-lb bombs. (USAF)

light bombers relentlessly smashed bridges over the Seine and Loire Rivers, attacked railway yards and communications centres and destroyed fuel and ammunition supply points serving the Germans along the entire Allied front in Normandy.

On 22 June a massive air bombing assault, including all available fighter-bombers, was launched against German fortifications and entrenched troops defending Cherbourg. The air attack went off moderately well and shook up the defending forces considerably. The medium bombers did excellent work and were properly employed. When the plan for the air operation of 22 June at Cherbourg was drawn up, it was acknowledged that the use of fighter-bombers in such a role would not contribute materially to the effectiveness of the air assault, particularly in view of the lack of adequate communications between the forces in Normandy and the bulk of the participating air units which were then still based in Britain. By 24 July eighteen fighter-bomber and reconnaissance groups of the 9th Air Force were fully operational from fifteen bases in Normandy and additional airfields were under construction for a reconnaissance group and four light or medium bomber groups.

On 9 August Captain Darrell R. Lindsey in the 394th Bomb Group led thirty-three Marauders against the railroad bridge at L'Isle Adam, one of the last Seine bridges still serviceable. Coming over enemy territory the formation was buffeted by heavy and accurate AA (anti-aircraft) fire, but by skilful evasive action Captain Lindsey eluded much of the enemy flak and brought the Marauders successfully into their bomb run. At this point his right engine received a direct hit and burst into flames, and the plane was hurled out of formation. Captain Lindsey brilliantly manoeuvred back into the lead position without disrupting the flight and then, fully aware his gasoline tanks might explode at any moment, he elected to continue leading the bomb run. Fire was streaming from his right engine and his right wing was half enveloped with flames as he took the formation over the target and dropped with excellent effect.

Immediately after bombs away Captain Lindsey gave the order for the crew to parachute from the now doomed B-26. With magnificent coolness and extraordinary piloting skill he held the swiftly descending plane in a steady glide until all but one of the crew beside himself had safely jumped. The last man to leave the plane was the bombardier. The entire right wing was now in flames and the bombardier offered to lower the wheels so Captain Lindsey might escape from the nose. Realising this might throw the aircraft into a spin and jeopardise the bombardier's chances of escape, Captain Lindsey refused the offer. He held the plane as steady as he could while the bombardier jumped and a bare moment later, before he could leave the controls, the right gas tank exploded. The aircraft, sheathed in fire and its gallant pilot still in the cockpit, plummeted down in a steep dive and exploded on contact with the ground. For his supreme courage (which saved the lives of one of the other eight men who had been in the bomber) Captain Darrell R. Lindsey was awarded the Medal of Honor.

Late in August IX Bomber Command moved four tactical groups from Britain to France in order to extend their range and to permit more frequent bombardment operations by taking advantage of the more favourable weather conditions on the continent. In late August and September the stretching of Allied lines of communication and the stiffening of German resistance at the Siegfried Line slowed the pace of the Allied advance until the battle turned into generally static warfare, which persisted until the German counter-offensive in

December. During this period, in addition to carrying out air operations diminished only because of weather, the 9th Air Force moved its forces into positions from which they could strike most effectively and at the shortest range against the enemy in his homeland. The capture of large numbers of partially demolished German airfields in the area near and east of Paris made it possible for IX Engineer Command to provide fields not only for air supply and evacuation behind the advance and for the basing of nearly all fighter and reconnaissance groups east of Laon, but also for the movement of the remaining seven medium bomber groups of IX Bomber Command from England to the Paris area. In October 1944 two P-61 night fighter squadrons were transferred from the Air Defence Command to the IX and XIX Tactical Air Commands. There they were armed with HVAR – High Velocity Aerial Rocket(s) – in addition to their 20-mm cannon, and dispatched on offensive night intruder operations as well as primarily defensive night fighter assignments.

On 9 October 1944 over 1,000 heavies struck at two marshalling yards and an engine plant at Mainz and bombed Koblenz, Gustavsburg, Schweinfurt and two targets of opportunity in western Germany. Nineteen fighter groups including two in the 9th Air Force provided support. On 4 November more than 1,000 heavies operating in six forces attacked synthetic oil plants, oil refineries and benzol plants at Bottrop, Gelsenkirchen, Hamburg, Harburg, Misburg and Neunkirchen. Seventeen fighter groups including a 9th Air Force group provided support on 9 November when over 1,100 heavies in conjunction with 9th Air Force aircraft hit targets in the Metz and Thionville area as the US Third Army forces launched a full-scale attack on Metz. On Christmas Eve 1944 the 8th Air Force was able to mount its largest single attack in history with 2,034 heavies participating. In addition, 500 RAF and 9th Air Force bombers participated in this, the greatest single aerial armada the world has ever seen. The 1st Division would be involved in a direct tactical assault on airfields in the Frankfurt area and on lines of communication immediately behind the German 'bulge'. Overall, the Christmas Eve raids were effective and severely hampered von Rundstedt's lines of communication. The cost in aircraft, though, was high. Many crashed during their return over England as drizzle and overcast played havoc with landing patterns.

As early as 31 December fighter-bombers of the 9th Air Force,

A-20 over the D-Day invasion area.

some of which were operating from newly completed airfields in the vicinity of Metz and Maastricht, were cooperating intimately with the ground forces in a new offensive to drive the Germans out of their area of penetration. Practically cut off from their supply sources, driven from the roads in the daylight and bombed incessantly in villages within the salient, the enemy forces soon decided to retreat to prepared defensive positions rather than to try to maintain the tenuously held captured area. Although this retreat never turned into a rout it was grossly expensive for the enemy, since fighter-bombers destroyed thousands of vehicles on the various main and secondary roads leading out of the bulge. In one particularly well-coordinated air force operation medium bombers on 22 January destroyed a bridge crossing the Our River at Dasburg and caused an enormous traffic jam on the west bank of the river. Fighter-bombers, attacking continuously until darkness, destroyed or damaged that day alone almost 3,000 motor and armoured vehicles among the concentrations created by the bridge attack. By the end of January all ground lost in the counter-offensive had been recovered by the American ground forces.

After the threat in the Ardennes had been eliminated the First and Third Armies resumed their drive toward the Rhine. All three phases of the tactical mission were discharged by the tactical air commands. IX Tactical Air Command continued to cooperate with the First Army in the comparatively slow drive to the western banks of the Roer. Fighter-bombers of XIX Tactical Air Command, frequently striking within sight of the front lines as the Third Army crossed the Prüm, the Saar and the Moselle, helped form and reduce enemy pockets in the 130-square-mile area of the Moselle-Saar triangle guarding the approaches to Trier. Further north the formation of a huge new pocket was begun by a series of planned attacks on key communications points around the perimeter of the Ruhr Valley. This interdiction campaign, one of the most important preoccupations of the 9th Air Force during February and March, was carried out largely by medium and light bombers, while fighter-bombers flew mostly against moving vehicles on railway lines and roads approaching the Ruhr from the east, north, and south. One of the most remarkable phases of the general interdiction campaign came on 22 February 1945, when all available Allied aircraft combined in Operation *Clarion*, a series of simultaneous attacks designed to paralyse the entire railway system in western Germany, with particular emphasis on the areas east of the Ruhr, east of Coblenz and in the Palatinate. The planning and execution of the 9th Air Force part of this massive assault were superb and resulted in one of its most successful days of operations during the entire war. The 9th Bombardment Division divided its bombers into small formations, which struck at sixty-one bridges, junctions, sidings, and railway yards. Forty-one of these formations dropped to low levels after the bombing, to strafe German targets of opportunity on the roads and railway lines. This operation and subsequent operations ensured that the German railway system in the 9th Air Force sector of responsibility was of little use to the Wehrmacht.

On 23 February, coordinating their air assault with the ground troops which were launching a heavy attack across the Roer River, medium and light bombers were effectively employed against communications centres and railway yards and contributed materially to the inability of the enemy to marshal his forces effectively for a counter-attack or for a coherent defence. Attacks on fortified towns in connection with the Roer crossings also had good effect and resulted in restriction of the enemy's use of artillery against the crossings. Fighter-bombers carried out particularly active operations throughout the period of this offensive, literally withering enemy attempts to set up road blocks and maintain defensive stands. Fighter-bombers attacked with everything they had, including fire bomb HE (high explosive) bombs, fragmentation clusters, rockets, and eight 5 G-

B-26s bombing a target on the continent of Europe.

Using a heater to warm the engine of a B-26.

calibre machine guns. Another contribution of these aircraft was to permit troops to concentrate for the jump-off without interference from enemy air.

On 2 March the First Army reached the Rhine and soon after crossed the Ludendorff Bridge at Remagen and swiftly established a bridgehead east of the Rhine. Fighter-bombers by this time were experienced in the defence of precarious bridgeheads and when the Germans ranged Me 262s, Ju 87s and heavy artillery against First Army elements on the eastern bank of the Rhine, IX Tactical Air Command immediately established an air patrol over the area, to cooperate with massed anti-aircraft responsible for the close air defence of the bridge. Meanwhile, other fighter-bombers swept ahead to attack all possible bases from which Germans were taking off against the bridgehead. A typical attack was against the Lippe airfield on 15 March, which resulted in the destruction or damaging of more than 100 enemy aircraft on the ground. As a further safeguard to the preservation of this all-important bridgehead First Army and IX Tactical Air Command transmitted a request to air force-army group headquarters that medium bombers carry out an interdiction campaign against railway targets which might support German forces in the bridgehead area. These operations, most of them carried out by instrument bombing through heavy clouds, helped weaken enemy opposition to the First Army and minimised the movement of German reserves to the critical area.

On 19 March fighter-bombers of the XIX Tactical Air Command were sent to destroy the headquarters of the German Commander-in-Chief, West, at Ziegenberg, near Bad Nauheim. This old castle, where Hitler and von Rundstedt planned the Ardennes breakthrough, was attacked by P-47s during the noon meal hour, from minimum altitudes. The 1,000-lb and 500-lb GP (general purpose) bombs and 150-gallon napalm fire bombs launched by two squadrons put the entire headquarters, including the castle and adjacent buildings, out of any future use. General von Rundstedt, following his capture, complained: 'Allied planes not only shattered our supply lines but they carried the war right home by hitting the headquarters at Bad Nauheim.'

On 21 March preparatory air operations for the forthcoming (23 March) crossing of the lower Rhine by Allied ground forces began. In morning raids, 1,254 bombers in conjunction with aircraft of the RAF and 9th Air Force attacking other targets, bombed ten airfields in north-west Germany, a tank factory at Plauen and a marshalling yard at Reichenbach. The missions of 21 March were the start of a massive four-day assault on the *Luftwaffe*, with 42,000 sorties being made over German airspace. The second Rhine crossing was made easily and speedily by the Third Army on the night of 22 March. The following morning fighter-bombers of XIX Tactical Air Command initiated the usual programme of area cover and direct cooperation and kept in the air from first light to dusk. A number of German planes were shot down when the *Luftwaffe* attempted a slight revival of its aerial campaign against the Third Army. However, fighter-bombers were primarily useful against German gun positions, troop concentrations, command installations and vehicles. Toward the end of March the battleground was rapidly shifting east of the Rhine to the heart of Germany and eastward to Czechoslovakia and Austria. The third

Rhine crossing was made by two airborne divisions of the First Allied Airborne Army, which were dropped in the Wesel area on 23 March as fighter-bombers flew thousands of sorties against German flak positions in the drop zones and protected the long procession of tugs and gliders. Not one plane of any description was lost to air attack during the airborne crossing – an indication both of the effectiveness of the escort and of the success of recent attacks on Me 262 jet aircraft and other airfields by the 8th and 9th Air Forces and the RAF. With three Rhine bridgeheads at widely separated points the immobile and shattered German army was unable to put up any effective resistance and Allied ground forces made swift progress on all fronts. The 9th and First Armies closed the Ruhr pocket on 1 April, some time after the great industrial valley had been rendered practically useless to the enemy because of the disorganisation of the entire German transportation system. The 9th Air Force assisted in reducing stubborn enemy elements within the pocket, as fighter-bombers kept pace with the 9th Army break-through in which some ground units gained 200 miles in two weeks. Fighter-bombers flew principally armoured column cover, closely coordinating air attacks with ground effort, enabling the attacking forces speedily to reduce road blocks, overcome strongpoints and occupy defended buildings and field fortifications. Defensively, the same planes flew protective patrols which were particularly important during build-up stages when heavy concentrations of Allied armour were vulnerable to air attack. Tactical reconnaissance aircraft informed forward ground units of the location of demolished bridges and of resistance pockets until the 9th Army reached the west bank of the Elbe as the Russians arrived on the east bank. During this period the combined American air forces added the final touches to the destruction of the German Air Force, which by this time was concentrated on relatively few airfields and was almost completely grounded by the critical fuel shortage. In one seven-day period the Eighth, Ninth and First Tactical Air Forces destroyed or damaged more than 3,400 enemy aircraft on the ground.

During the twenty-five months of its existence the 9th Air Force grew from a tiny nucleus to over 200,000 personnel in forty-five combat groups and a vast selection of non-combat units, flying over 1,100 bomber aircraft, a huge number of fighters and 3,000 troop-carrying aircraft. The personnel of the 9th Air Force could rightly be proud of their efforts and attainments. On 15 July 1945 the Field Commander of the 12th Army Group, General Omar N. Bradley, stated:

> The axiomatic requirement that victory can only be achieved by the attainment of supremacy on the land, sea and in the air has never been so fully proven as in this total defeat of an enemy who never controlled the sea, who tried to substitute strategic artillery for a defeat in the air, and whose armed forces were crushed and homeland over-run by the combined power of our supremacy in all these three elements.

Marauders in the 322nd Bomb Group led by *Clark's Little Pill* taxi out at Andrews Field. *(USAF)*

PFC Barbara O'Brien, a WAC at IX Bomber Command, touches up the artwork for *Jolly Roger*, which would fly 130 missions in the 323rd Bomb Group.*(USAF)*

B-26B-45-MA 42-95808 O8-C *Idiot's Delight* in the 575th Bomb Squadron, 391st Bomb Group. *(USAF)*

THE AIRFIELDS

1

ANDREWS FIELD
(Great Saling)
(Station 485)

The third bomber airfield in Essex to be completed, Great Saling was also the first to be constructed by US army engineers. The 819th Engineer Battalion (Aviation) commenced work on the site in July 1942. The runways were completed by November and during some periods of fine weather, work continued during darkness with the aid of screened lighting. While the basic airfield itself was declared complete by mid-January 1943, there was still much work to be done on other facilities and in March additional help was obtained from another engineer battalion. Great Saling was considered ready for operational use in April 1943 and a month later, on 21 May, it was officially renamed Andrews Field after Lieutenant General Frank M. Andrews, Commanding General of the US Army in the ETO, who had been killed in a B-24 Liberator crash in Iceland on 3 May. A standard bomber airfield to Class A specification, Andrews Field had a 6,000 foot main runway and two 4,200 foot runways. Fifty-one hardstandings consisted of forty-six standard loops, four large loops and one pan. There were two dispersed T2 hangars and accommodation for 2,841 personnel. The base was first home to the 8th Air Force's 96th Bomb Group and its B-17s in May 1943, which were replaced by the 322nd Bomb Group with B-26 Marauders the following month. The 422nd Bomb Group was commanded by Colonel Glen C. Nye and the group became known as 'Nye's Annihilators'. They would remain at the base for longer than any other Marauder group's stay at one location.

On 17 July the 322nd Bomb Group was officially put back on combat status and on 29 July the 322nd made its second ETO 'debut'

B-26B Marauders in the 322nd Bomb Group taxi out at Andrews Field in September 1943. *(USAF)*

when the Group taxied out for the mission to Woensdrecht. *Two Way Ticket*, the last Marauder to take off, lost its right engine on take-off and crashed. *The Wolf* and 1st Lieutenant Glenn F. Zimmerman's crew in the 553rd Squadron failed to return from the raid. Only one gunner survived. On 31 July eighteen B-26s were sent to bomb Triqueville airfield. Thirteen aircraft got their bombs away. Lieutenant Colonel Robert C. Fry, who had gained some early fame by landing a B-26 on one engine, lost an engine on the mission. Forced to shut it down completely, Fry headed for home, where he again made a successful emergency landing. Fry went on to make more 'engine out' landings, his total of six being rumoured to be higher than that of any other B-26 pilot. Robert Fry flew combat with the 322nd until the ill-fated night mission of 7/8 July 1944 when he was shot down and became a PoW.

Marauders in the 452nd Bomb Squadron, 322nd Bomb Group, being prepared for a mission at Andrews Field. The nearest aircraft is 41-31878. *(USAF)*

Easter Sunday service, 1944, probably at the 322nd's base at Andrews Field. (*USAF*)

On 4 August the 322nd went to the shipyards at Le Trait, near Rouen. The thirty-three Marauders that reached the target area dropped sixty 500-lb GP bombs from 11,000 feet and hit a power station, boiler rooms and manufacturing areas plus several vessels dry-docked and on slipways. The raid, which left the entire waterfront area wreathed in smoke, was an outstanding example of precision bombing, with no resulting crew casualties or aircraft damage, despite reaction from the flak defences. On the 9th, the 322nd and 386th flew to St-Omer only to find the target airfield obscured by cloud and radar-predicted flak found the bombers' altitude, putting holes in eleven Marauders and wounding six men. On 18 August the 322nd and 386th Groups were briefed to bomb Ypres and Woensdrecht airfields in

B-26B 41-31819 *Mild and Bitter* in the 322nd Bomb Group on its fiftieth mission on 7 January 1944. (*USAF*)

B-26B 41-31819 *Mild and Bitter* **in the 322nd Bomb Group was the first Marauder to complete 100 missions from England. Named after a popular British brew, it was signed by air and ground crews before going home to the States for a war bond sales tour.** (*S. Piet Coll via J. Scutts*)

Belgium while P-47 fighter sweeps were flown in support of the mediums. For the bombers these were secondary targets, as the primary – Lille-Vendeville airfield – could not be reached due to bad weather. No American aircraft were lost from either force, although thirty-one B-26s returned with varying degrees of battle damage. On 19 August unseasonal weather brought about a smaller-than-planned attack on enemy aerodromes: the 323rd sent thirty-six B-26s to Amiens-Glisy, while the 387th despatched thirty-five of its Marauders

A Barber Greene Mobile Asphalt plant used by the 819th Engineer Battalion (Aviation) at Andrews Field. (*USAF*)

PFC Ben Rosenblatt in the 322nd Bomb Group took a series of photos of Marauders during his first combat mission in August 1943. *(USAF)*

to Poix. The 322nd's target was to have been Bryas Sud, but thick cloud cover caused the mission to be abandoned. On the afternoon of 25 August, two minutes after the last of the 387th's B-26s left, the thirty-six 322nd Bomb Group aircraft were above Triqueville in the third attack on this aerodrome within a month. At least sixty-five craters were made by the bombs going down across the airfield from west to east. A large hangar in the western dispersal was destroyed by a direct hit and another severely damaged, also by a direct hit, and there were several near misses. In what was identified as an oil-storage area, a workshop was swept by fire, and there were observable craters in road ways and taxiways in the northern dispersal area. Other buildings were also damaged. Flak holed two Marauders but without causing any crew injuries.

On 16 October, in common with the other B-26 groups of VIII Air Support Command, the 322nd Bomb Group became part of the 9th Air Force. In May 1943 the 322nd had been the first B-26 group to enter combat from the UK and had flown more than forty missions when it became part of the 9th Air Force. On 5 November when 150 Marauders were dispatched to bomb Mimoyecques in France, the site of concrete earthworks for the so-called 'V-3' long range gun, two B-26s were lost. One, in the 322nd and piloted by 1st Lieutenant H. M. Price, was hit by flak that exploded in the radio compartment, setting it on fire. Price pulled his Marauder out of formation so as not to

Close-up of the autographed starboard side of *Mild and Bitter*. (*S. Piet Coll via J. Scutts*)

endanger the other planes and kept it under control despite the blazing fire until three or four men baled out. Then the plane disintegrated in mid-air. On 26 November when 198 Marauders were dispatched, the primary target for the 322nd and 386th Bomb Groups was Rosières-en-Santerre. However, the landing ground at Roye Amy was identified by mistake and bombed.

On 11 December 1943 Andrews Field was attacked by the *Luftwaffe* but little damage was done. In December 1943 US-built examples of *Oboe* navigation equipment had begun to arrive in the UK. These sets were installed in B-26s intended for a new unit, the 1st Pathfinder

819th Engineer Battalion (Aviation) at work at Andrews Field. (*USAF*)

Paul Shannon's crew who flew *Mild and Bitter* on its 100th mission on 9 May 1944. The ship was named by her Texan crew chief William Stuart after the B-26 had flown about forty missions. (*USAF*)

Squadron (Provisional). The 8th Air Force was already using *Gee-H*, but the 9th Air Force clearly needed its own electronic aids in its own medium bombers in order to penetrate the troublesome cloud cover. The 1st Pathfinder Squadron (Provisional) was formally activated at Andrews Field on 13 February 1944, equipped with B-26s carrying the British *Oboe* Mk II radar blind-bombing device. Its first fifteen crews, including Captain Robert A. Porter the CO, were drawn from the five Marauder groups in the ETO. Porter was a veteran of the first Ijmuiden mission with the 322nd Bomb Group and had been instrumental in forming the special squadron which, primarily, would provide bad weather leads for all groups in IX Bomber Command. The Pathfinders would also drop bundles of 'Window', the bundles of tiny aluminium strips cut to the wavelength of German radars, to help neutralise radar-predicted flak. The 1st Pathfinder Squadron flew its first mission on 21 February when eighteen PFF ships rendezvoused with 200-plus B-26s and led them in the bombing of Coxyde-Furnes airfield. The pathfinders were the only element that was able to bomb, while the rest were forced to return early.

Operations continued apace during the winter and spring and on 9 May 1944 *Mild and Bitter* in the 452nd Squadron became the first B-

WAC Virginia Reynolds paints the twenty-fifth bomb symbol on a B-26 with the 'class' name of *Stirling Hutchens & Company Flyin' Circus*. It was flown by Lieutenant John 'Bull' Stirling. (*USAF*)

This B-26 in the 322nd Bomb Group made it back from the disastrous night mission on 7/8 July 1944 to attack the *Noball* headquarters at Chateau de Ribeaucourt when 'Nye's Annihilators' lost nine Marauders shot down by Bf 110s of NJG 6. Colonel Nye was killed in the Korean War flying a B-26 Invader. (*USAF*)

A gunner in the 322nd Bomb Group points to a shell hole in the nose of a 322nd Bomb Group Marauder following the mission on 7/8 July 1944. (*USAF*)

Second Lieutenant Salvo was a fox terrier carried by Captain Hugh Fletcher, the bombardier on the crew of B-26 *Jezabelle* in the 452nd Bomb Squadron at Andrews Field. Salvo who reportedly flew two combat missions, was issued with 'dog tags' of course, and a parachute and life vest made from surplus material. (*USAF*)

26 flying from England to complete 100 combat missions and personnel threw a party. The aircraft was flown on the momentous mission by Lieutenant Paul Shannon, who had first flown this aircraft on 12 August 1943. Shannon recalled that:

> ...all the flak missed us by a safe margin. *Mild and Bitter* has often been called the 'luckiest ship in the 9th Air Force' having collected less than 50 flak holes, most of them small ones. Only once has battle damage kept her on the ground – a few days ago, when repairs on an electric line required about four hours, which wasn't enough time between missions...altogether she has hit military objectives in northern France 44 times, airfields 38 times and railway yards 14 times.

Mild and Bitter was taken off missions to make a triumphant return to the US to encourage AAF recruiting and sell war bonds. Not far behind *Mild and Bitter* were other 9th Air Force Marauders nearing the 100-mission mark. As the oldest serving group, the 322nd had at least half a dozen B-26s nearing a century. They included *'Lil Porkchop, Clark's*

Little Pill, *Bluebeard II*, *Pickled-Dilly*, *Sarah E* and *Idiot's Delight*. *Flak Bait*, then nearing 100 missions, survived to the end of hostilities with 202 missions completed; the only US bomber involved in combat over Europe to exceed the 200 mark.

In the run-up to D-Day the PFF B-26s led formations of Marauders against front-line airfields in northern France. On the afternoon of 21 May when Abbeville/Drucat airfield was the target, four PFF Marauders led thirty B-26s in the 322nd and thirty-two in the 391st in the bombing of the airfield. This operation was well protected by the 9th Air Force's two Mustang groups – the 354th (which put up forty-three aircraft) and 363rd (eighteen). Although the bombardiers had some difficulty with 9/10 cloud cover at the target the force dropped 127 500-lb GP bombs on the airfield as well as scattering leaflets. Having crossed into France between Cayeux and Le Treport, the B-26s exited over Pointe de St Quentin to avoid the coastal flak.

On the night of 22/23 May 1944 the 322nd Bomb Group dispatched sixteen Marauders on a night bombing mission to Beaumont le Roger

A 322nd Bomb Group B-26 coming off the target at Neuenburg railway bridge over the Rhine east of the Belfort Gap on 19 November 1944. The destruction of the bridge greatly assisted the US Seventh Army's offensive to drive the retreating German army out of France. (USAF)

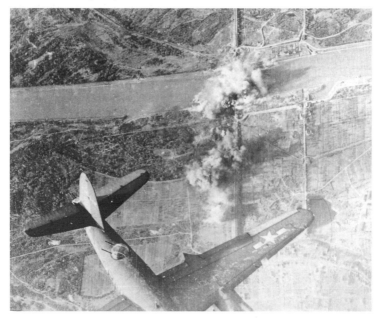

Flying Ben Willis' *Truman Committee* in the 322nd Bomb Group (Willis was the 449th Bomb Squadron CO) on the mission to a *Noball* site on 28 February 1944. Shell splinters wounded Frank Remmele (the pilot) wounding him, and killed the bombardier. In 1941 a Senate Special Committee chaired by Senator (later president) Harry S. Truman stated that if the B-26 were not given a bigger wing Truman would have the contract terminated. The wing was extended but after the disastrous mission to Ijmuiden on 17 May 1943 Truman called for production of the aircraft to be cancelled forthwith. The USAAF postponed movement of further B-26 groups to England and at one time moves almost led to the termination of B-26 production altogether. *(USAF)*

airfield which the Group had also attacked that day. The 322nd had been practising night flying for several weeks and this attack marked the first time Marauders based in the UK had executed a night mission in force. The requirement was for selected crews to bomb with pinpoint accuracy at night, from between 4,500 and 7,000 feet, using flares and under pathfinder direction. Fifteen B-26s bombed the primary target on target indicators dropped by pathfinders. Crews reported the target was well illuminated and that bombs fell right between the target indicators. 'Nye's Annihilators' received special commendation from Major General Samuel E. Anderson of IX Bomber Command who said, '(this) is the first instance in which B-26 aircraft have been used for night combat. I congratulate you and your Group for this outstanding accomplishment in the history of the 322nd Group and of IX Bomber Command.' During the mission two

Marauders were attacked by a single enemy night fighter but the fighter made only one pass and caused no damage.

Allen W. Stephens was awakened at two o'clock in the morning on 6 June. Later, the briefing officer announced: 'Today is D-Day. The invasion has already started and we are going to try to prevent the Germans from bringing up reinforcements. The weather is very bad and we may bomb by radar.'

This was Stephens' twenty-first mission and take-off was at 0420 hours. It was still dark. A steady rain was falling and they could hardly see to taxi, much less fly. But there was no holding back and they poured on the coals, taking off at twenty-second intervals between shifts. By the time they cleared the end of the runway, they could barely see the lights of the plane ahead of them. They climbed on instruments and when they broke out on top of the cloudbank, they could see B-26s and all kinds of other planes circling around. Stephens recalled that it was 'really a beautiful sight'. By following prearranged signals, Stephen's B-26 tacked onto their squadron leader and subsequently they were on their way across the Channel. He felt part of the spearhead of the invasion, entering the coast of France near Cherbourg over *Utah* Beach. His Group's targets were coastal guns

At Andrews Field Albert Smith looks on as one of his crew points out the symbol of a truck destroyed by *Geraldine*, which returned with flak damage and bellied in at the airfield. The parents of the real Geraldine returned the naming gesture by having their baby son christened Martin. (*USAF*)

Back from leading the 322nd Bomb Group's second box to the E-boat and S-boat docking facilities and pens at Ijmuiden on 26 March 1944, when 338 B-26s were dispatched, Othel Turner (cigarette in mouth) and Captain Louis Sebille (cigarette in hand) talk with other crew members of the lead ship (41-31975 ER-R). Both pilots flew on the first Ijmuiden mission in 1943, as had Lieutenant Ben Tillman, bombardier (second from left) and Sergeant Harold Baker (far right). Gove Celio, who led the first element, and Howard M. Possen, who led the second box, were also veterans of the first Ijmuiden mission. Celio lost an engine to flak and crash-landed in England. Two S-boats were sunk and only slight damage was caused to the pens and dock area after the formation leader dropped his bombs short and many crews following did the same. Louis Sebille who flew sixty-eight missions on Marauders, was killed flying a F-51 Mustang in the Korean War in August 1950 when his actions resulted in the award of a posthumous Medal of Honor. (USAF)

B-26C 41-31773 *Flak Bait* in the 449th Bomb Squadron with three other 322nd Bomb Group Marauders including the bare metal 42-107664 PN-A *Je Reviens* (I Return), which lived up to its name and completed sixty-nine missions. Above *Flak Bait* is 43-34371 PN-X. Bringing up the rear is PN-D 41-31822. (USAF)

and blockhouses along the beach, which they were to hit in collaboration with shelling by naval vessels. His was among the very first aircraft to hit the invasion target.

On D-Day 'Nye's Annihilators' was one of the key units in the opening bombardment and the 322nd Bomb Group dispatched three boxes of sixteen B-26s each, including a pathfinder for each box during the early morning hours. Only two Marauders of the first box succeeded in dropping their bombs on a battery at Ouistreham. In the second box, seven were abortive due to weather while nine bombed the second gun position at Ouistreham through 7 to 9/10ths clouds. The third box hit the Montfarville gun positions with excellent results. There was no enemy air opposition and no flak damage was sustained. *Pickled-Dilly* flew with a crew of only three men. The pilot, 1st Lieutenant William L. Adams, did his own radio and navigation work as well as flying the Marauder, co-pilot 1st Lieutenant Carl O. Steen took over the bombardier's duties while the bombardier, Staff Sergeant C. W. Holland, went back and handled the tail guns. *Pickled-Dilly* put its bombs right on the target. *Pickled-Dilly* would complete 105 combat missions before being lost on its 106th mission on the night of 7/8 July on the raid on the *Noball* headquarters at Chateau de Ribeaucourt.

As he moved in toward the beaches, Allen W. Stephens and the crew of his B-26 Marauder could see an armada of invasion vessels in the Channel below, their courses converging toward the several invasion beaches. Stephens had the surging feeling that he was sitting in on the greatest show ever staged – one that would make world history. As they flew nearer to the target, that feeling increased to exhilaration and excitement. He saw hundreds upon hundreds of ships

Major John C. Ruse, 449th Bomb Squadron CO, congratulates Sergeant Clair G. Goodrich of the ground crew after *Flak Bait*'s 200th mission. (USAF)

B-26C 41-31773 *Flak Bait* in the 449th Bomb Squadron, 322nd Bomb Group, flew 202 missions and the fuselage is now preserved in the Smithsonian in Washington DC. (*USAF*)

moving toward the coast of France and when he approached the target area, he could see their big naval guns shelling the coast. The Germans were not idle, however, as they threw heavy barrages at the landing craft. Stephens saw one large ship going down but still throwing shells at the coast. He saw hundreds of discarded parachutes that had been thrown off by paratroopers who had landed simultaneously with the other attacks. He saw one B-26 Marauder explode in mid-air near the target area. Stephens' group went through the heaviest concentration of anti-aircraft fire he had yet seen. Tracers and flak explosions were so thick that it looked impossible to get through without being hit, especially knowing that for every tracer there were six other rounds. The barrage literally filled the air all around and the flak explosions made the air alive with fire. On the beachhead, there was a tremendous wall of smoke all along the shore where the bombs and the shells were exploding. The landing craft were moving up as the Marauders turned off the target area after dropping their bombs. Every move was timed to the split second. Stephen's B-26s went in at 4,500 feet on this first mission and their bombs went away at 0630 hours, the precise time planned.

By July the Group was attacking targets throughout France. In clear moonlight on 7/8 July 'Nye's Annihilators' dispatched thirty-two B-26s plus three pathfinders to attack the *Noball* headquarters at Chateau de Ribeaucourt. Earlier in the day the *Maquis* who carried out an attack on the headquarters sent confirmation to England that the *château* housed Flak Regiment 155 (W) and was staffed by groups of officers and technicians who directed the launching of V-1s against southern England. The enemy reported the formation from approximately the time it passed in over the coast and it was picked up by searchlights and the flak opened up. In the Oisemont area ten miles into enemy territory, attacks by Messerschmitt Bf 110s of NJG 6 began. From then until the formation was out over the Channel on the way home, twenty night fighters were active against the Marauders, over half of them making firing passes. Bomber gunners reported fourteen attacks on their formation within the space of a few minutes. NJG 6 claimed

B-26 42-107685 ER-V of the 450th Bomb Squadron in invasion stripes. (USAF)

fourteen bombers (miss-identifying them as 'Wellingtons'), the first at 2210 hours. Two of the fighters, one the victim of German flak, were claimed destroyed but nine B-26s were lost, two damaged beyond repair and three slightly damaged (two by flak). Twenty-three B-26s bombed individually, dropping 39.5 tons of bombs from 6,500 to 9,000 feet. Most of the night fighter attacks came from the rear, low. Enemy flak and searchlight defences co-operated with the fighters and the flak ceased when a bomber was coned. Flares were also reported in use to illuminate the B-26s for attack by fighters. The single-engine fighters were mostly FW 190s and the twin-engined aircraft were Bf 110s and Ju 88s. The distinction of being the first American gunner in the ETO to destroy an enemy aircraft on a night mission went to Sergeant Kenneth M. Locke. The engineer-gunner returned the fire of a single-engined fighter that came in at seven o'clock and the enemy aircraft caught fire and went down out of control, enveloped in flames.

One of the B-26s flying the mission was *Homesick*, piloted by 1st Lieutenant Frank M. Cookson. On the bomb run the middle bomb hung up and on their way down the other bombs bounced off it, creating a terrible and frightening noise through the Marauder. A Ju 88 picked out *Homesick* and made four determined passes, aided by a strong concentration of searchlights that coned the Marauder all the way. In three passes the Ju 88 nearly picked *Homesick* apart with its 20-mm cannon. On its fourth pass it knocked out the top turret but not before Staff Sergeant J. K. Brandemihl, the gunner, aided by Sergeant Robert E. Johnson, the tail gunner, scored direct hits on it. The Ju 88 burst into flames and went out of control. Brandemihl, who was injured in the leg when his top turret was shot out, left his position, applied a tourniquet to the injury and staggered forward to the cockpit for further medical aid. Behind him the waist gunner and tail gunner, believing the shattered plane to be out of control, baled out over enemy territory. Later, the waist gunner's flak suit was found peppered with shell fragments and both waist gun barrels had large holes shot through them. As it returned across the Channel, *Homesick* had half its rudder surface shot off, its rudder and elevator trim tabs smashed, hydraulic reservoir, generators and top turret shot out, and the entire electrical system seriously impaired from direct hits. The B-26 managed to reach RAF Tangmere where it crash-landed without further injury to the crew. *Homesick* had come home, but for the last time; it was beyond repair. Another B-26 made it home but was badly damaged when its landing gear collapsed on touchdown. The 322nd had bombed on the

Flak bait in formation with PN-X

pathfinders' signal but the *château* was not hit.

Lieutenant Richard S. Bailey of Binghamton, New York, a twenty-two-year old pilot in the 322nd Bomb Group, said:

Some of the boys cried at the briefings before we went out on night missions. Some came in drunk and others carried on something awful. The Surgeon and the chaplain scurried around trying to buck them up. That Pas de Calais *No ball* area was really tough and the boys would say, 'Let them send the damned rockets over – they're not firing at us!' But they went out anyway and did the job the best they knew how. We bitched to beat hell about night missions. We didn't have any radar on our planes to detect enemy planes and they did have radars. And once a searchlight caught you – you had to dive to the deck to escape and the ground might be closer than you thought. On that third mission we lost nine of the thirty-six planes that went out. Someone screwed up and the RAF had just been over the territory so all the enemy fighters and flak were set for us.

Despite the disaster, night missions by B-26s continued. Other B-26 groups began night pathfinder training so that they could all fly a rota of night sorties for one month at a time. The 323rd Group was then training selected crews and would fly its first such operational mission in August. The 322nd moved to Beauvais-Tillé (A-61) in France in the last week of September 1944. Andrews Field was immediately returned to RAF control on 1 October to provide a base for Mustang squadrons escorting Bomber Command daylight operations. At this time the airfield was also under consideration for extension of runways to house very heavy bombers. Mustang squadrons and Gloster Meteors flew from the airfield for a few months after the end of hostilities but by the end of 1945 the station was on care and maintenance and the following year local farmers were permitted to cultivate land around the runways. Hangars and other facilities were sold or removed and in the mid-1960s the runways and perimeter tracks were broken up for use as hardcore for road making. In 1973, one of the landowners, Clive Harvey, utilised the grass strip close to the site of the main runway for private flying. Three years later the Andrews Field Flying Club was formed.

2

BIRCH
(Station 149)

In August 1942 Birch was allocated to the 8th Air Force and land was requisitioned but construction did not begin until the 846th Engineer Battalion arrived the following summer. Their task was to lay a main concrete runway 6,000 feet long and two 4,200 feet long intersecting runways and build fifty loop-type hardstandings and erect two T2 hangars. In addition, on seven sites to the east largely Nissen hut accommodation was to be constructed to house 2,894 personnel. In October 1943 the 9th Air Force decided that it would base a fighter group at Birch in December but this did not take place because although the runways were then completed, work on the hardstandings

B-26 Marauder *Dee-Feater* in the 596th Bomb Squadron at Rivenhall passing Birch airfield in July 1944. The bomb store is off the north-east end of the airfield (top) and the domestic sites are to the south. In the foreground is the A12 road to Colchester. (*USAF*)

A Model 101 power grader of the 862nd Engineering Battalion (Aviation) at work on one of the 4,200-foot runways at Birch. (USAF)

had only just begun. The base was still lacking many facilities when the 410th Bomb Group, commanded by Colonel Ralph Rhudy and comprising the 644th, 645th, 646th and 647th Bomb Squadrons, arrived from the USA in the first week of April 1944. After only twelve days the Group personnel were transferred to Gosfield and Birch was left to the construction teams to continue their work. On 13 May low cloud, prolonged rain and poor visibility hindered the general clearing and preparation of the landing ground area and the US engineers were surprised to suddenly see four P-38 Lightnings in the 474th Fighter Group, 9th Air Force, land on one of the runways. They were returning from a combat mission to Warmwell but because of the appalling weather, decided to land at the first airfield they saw. Visibility was so poor they did not see the large amount of construction materials alongside the runways and they were fortunate to have landed long, missing obstructions at the end. These were probably the first combat aircraft to land at Birch and they were waved off by the engineers next day.

The 9th Air Force decided it had no need of Birch and the base was transferred to the 3rd Bomb Division, 8th Air Force, as a reserve airfield but after completion of construction work, no operational units were based here. Throughout the remainder of 1944 Birch was used only for the occasional exercise or acted as an emergency landing strip for aircraft low on fuel and battle-damaged bombers and fighters returning from combat missions on the continent. In September the airfield was set to become a base for C-47 groups in the 52nd Troop Carrier Wing in the Newark-Grantham area but this never materialised.

In March 1945 a large number of Horsa gliders were landed on the airfield and Dakotas of 48, 233 and 437 Squadrons, 46 Group RAF, arrived on detachment from Blakehill Farm and Down Ampney. On 24 March the Dakotas began taking off from Birch at 6.00 am, each towing a Horsa, a total of sixty tugs and sixty gliders being launched, delivering part of the British 6th Airborne Division in the crossing of the Rhine. Most Dakotas were directed to land at other bases following this operation and 46 Group withdrew from Birch during the next few days. Thereafter, the base was occupied by various RAF ground organisations and little further use was made of the airfield. In early post-war years, the housekeeping party was soon withdrawn, the base gradually dismantled and the runways broken up.

3

BOREHAM
(Station 161)

This airfield was constructed by US Army engineers on farmland lying between Boreham and Little Waltham villages. Although the site had been requisitioned in 1942 for a bomber airfield in the Air Ministry A grouping, the main construction work did not start until the following spring when, on 13 May, the 861st Engineer Battalion (Aviation) arrived to build a main runway of 6,000 feet and two of 4,200 feet with fifty loop-type hardstandings and erect two T2 hangars. The construction would include the complete removal of the eighty-six-acre Dukes Wood and new barracks were to house 2,658 personnel but bad weather hampered construction and when the first B-26 Marauders of the 394th Bomb Group arrived from the USA on 10 March 1944, some hardstandings and buildings were still not complete. The 394th

Lieutenant Jack Logan's B-26B *War Horse* in the 394th Bomb Group.
(R. M. Brown)

Air Chief Marshal Sir Trafford Leigh-Mallory talks to a mechanic working on B-26C-15 41-34946 *The Yankee Guerrilla* **during a visit to the 386th Bomb Group at Boreham.** *(USAF)*

Bomb Group was commanded by Colonel Thomas B. Hall and comprised the 584th, 585th, 586th and 587th Bomb Squadrons.

Clear conditions over Europe on the morning of 23 March enabled the Group to fly their first mission only twelve days after the majority of the Group arrived, when the target was Beaumont-le-Roger airfield. During a *Noball* mission to Bois de Esquerdes on 21 April, Captain William R. Schulte was leading a box formation which would drop on his bombardier's signal. Just before the target the Marauder was struck by flak and one engine was hit, requiring the pilot to feather the propeller, but he stayed in position and led his box over the target where bombs were dropped with excellent results. Then he slid out of

B-26 44-67822 K5-V in the 584th Bomb Squadron, 394th Bomb Group. *(USAF)*

the formation and returned to Boreham on one engine without further incident. Next day Colonel Thomas Hall, the CO, led his Group against targets in the city of Heuringhem. For one minute prior to bombs away, the formation was under intense, accurate anti-aircraft fire. Fifteen seconds before bomb release, Colonel Hall's B-26 was hit by flak, which caused extensive damage to the electrical system, the hydraulic system and the right engine. The G-box was destroyed and part of the left horizontal stabiliser was taken off. Only the electrical system damage prevented the bombardier from putting the formation's bombs on the target so he salvoed his bombs with poor results but the following formation laid their bombs right on the target. Coming out from the target and back across the Channel, Colonel Hall continued to lead his Group. Then, with his co-pilot seriously wounded, he pulled out and rushed the B-26 in to get medical help for him. On the ground they counted 264 holes in the Marauder.

In the weeks that followed, the 394th was repeatedly sent to bomb bridges in occupied France and the Low Countries. 'The Bridge Busters' as they became known, flew a total of ninety-six combat missions from Boreham, on which 5,453 tons (US) of bombs were dropped. On 10 May the 394th Bomb Group sent thirty-nine Marauders in six flights to the Creil marshalling yards. Sixty-eight tons were dropped with five of the flights scoring excellent results, but one flight commander was hit by flak and his B-26 went down. All six men baled out – one was killed, three made prisoners of war and two evaded capture and later returned to England. Creil was the most frequently attacked marshalling yard, being hit eleven times between 7 March and 22 May. After 10 May, the locomotive depot there was 70 per cent destroyed and the roundhouse demolished. Two further

B-26B 42-96074 *Ish-Tak-Ha-Ba* in the 584th Bomb Squadron, 394th Bomb Group. The Indian name means 'Sleepy Eye' and is also the name of a town in Minnesota where Lieutenant Martin Harter, the original pilot of this Marauder, came from. *(USAF)*

attacks in May put the yards 60 per cent out of action and further damaged the rails. Sixteen B-26s went missing in action from Boreham, almost all to enemy anti-aircraft fire. In order to increase its radius of combat action the four B-26 groups of the 98th Combat Bomb Wing moved south to occupy airfields in Hampshire and the 394th Bomb Group moved on 24 July to Holmsley South. In September 1944 Boreham was temporarily under the control of IX Troop Carrier Command as an advanced and emergency base for the airborne landings in Holland, but a glider mission from Boreham to a landing strip near Grave, scheduled for 26 September, was cancelled at the last minute because of predicted bad weather.

For a time the airfield was used by a small number of personnel of the Air Disarmament Command which carried out the occupation and disarming of *Luftwaffe* installations. They left in January 1945 and

Marauders of the 584th Bomb Squadron, 394th Bomb Group, at the unfinished airfield at Boreham on 14 March 1944. (*USAF*)

Boreham as construction work continues on 14 March 1944. The B-26 (left) is a 394th Bomb Group machine, which had only just arrived at the unfinished base. *(USAF)*

Boreham then passed to the RAF on 1 March. That same month the airfield was assigned to the IX Troop Carrier Command and on the 14th an advance party from the 315th Troop Carrier Group moved in and over eighty C-47s arrived on 22 March. Two days later they carried men of the British 6th Airborne Division in Operation *Varsity*, the airborne assault on the east bank of the Rhine. The Group was badly hit by the ground fire encountered, six of the C-47s being brought down and another seven so badly damaged that they had to make emergency landing in friendly territory.

Boreham airfield closed in early 1946 and Essex County Council used some of the Nissen huts on the domestic sites to house the homeless and the land was used by Co-Partnership Farms. That same year the West Essex Car Club developed the 4.76 kilometre perimeter track for motor racing which continued at Boreham until 1952. The Ford Motor Company bought the airfield in 1955 to use as a test facility for trucks and built twelve different test areas, including a rough road track of 2.4 kilometres. Boreham became the headquarters of Ford Motorsport of Europe.

BOXTED (Langham)
(Station 150)

Work on Boxted airfield began in the summer of 1942 with W. & C. French as the main contractor. The site, almost entirely in the parish of Langham, had a few of the barrack sites within the borough boundary of Colchester lying directly to the south. The main runway was 6,000 feet long and the two others were 4,200 feet with forty-four loop hardstandings, one large loop and six pans. Two T2 hangars – one on each side of the airfield – and two fuel dumps of 72,000-gallon capacity were also constructed and seven domestic sites accommodated 2,894 personnel.

The airfield was first occupied by the 386th Bomb Group with its

Staff Sergeant George W. Leonard (left) and Sergeant Robert L. Seager working on a 354th Fighter Group P-51B Mustang on 13 January 1944. (USAF)

Sergeant Marvin Lippoff eases a belt of 0.50-inch ammunition into the feed in the wing position of a 354th Fighter Group P-51B Mustang on 13 January 1944. *(USAF)*

Parafrags hung in multiples on P-51B wing racks for maximum impact. *(USAF)*

Colonel George R. Bickell was CO of 354th Fighter Group from 10 April 1944 to July 1945. *(USAF)*

B-26 Marauders in June 1943. The Group, which was later to take the name 'Crusaders', was commanded by forty-five-year-old Lieutenant Colonel Lester Maitland who had gained his wings in 1916. During the morning of 29 July the Group flew its first mission from Boxted when, escorted by 128 P-47s, the 386th made a feint towards the St-Omer region in an attempt to lure the *Luftwaffe* fighters away from the 323rd Bomb Group formation flying to Zeebrugge. One FW 190 was damaged in the single fighter action with the Thunderbolts. Late in the afternoon the 386th flew its first bombing mission, when twenty-four Marauders, six from each squadron, were dispatched to Woensdrecht airfield in Holland. At take-off time 1st Lieutenant Ray Williamson, piloting *Two-way Ticket*, cleared the perimeter and the aircraft's gear came up, but at less than 100 feet one engine suddenly died and Williamson crashed back down in a field across the road from the airfield. The crew were shaken but unhurt save for a few cuts and bruises. Over the Channel the 386th's crews rendezvoused with their Spitfire escort and headed into Holland. Several B-26s were damaged by flak but all made the target. However, haze intervened and only half the force were able to release their loads. As they turned away from Woensdrecht, the Marauders came under attack from eight FW 190s of JG 26 who miss-identified the bombers as Douglas Bostons. *Leutnant* Karl 'Charlie' Willius of 3rd *Staffel* shot down the B-26 flown by 1st Lieutenant Glenn F. Zimmerman, which spun into the Scheldt. One of the gunners was picked up by Dutch fishermen, only to be taken prisoner later. The American gunners were credited with six aircraft destroyed and five probables but the FW 190 piloted by *Leutnant*

Boxing bout at Boxted.(*USAF*)

Heinrich Sprinz which went down as he approached the B-26 formation was the only enemy loss. On 31 July the 386th flew two missions, its second mission target that day being Abbeville/Drucat airfield. Flak damaged five of the B-26s.

Often flying in large formations, the Marauders were especially valuable in attacks on enemy airfields at medium altitude and the 386th attacked V-1 and V-2 rocket sites and took part in the battle around Falaise. On 22 August 1943 Lieutenant Wilma T. Caldwell whose Marauder *Sad Ass* was hit in the bomb bay by FW 190s, putting one engine out of action, held the B-26 steady while his crew baled out. Four men managed to escape before the tanks exploded, breaking the Marauder in half. He was awarded a posthumous DSC.

The 386th Bomb Group moved to Great Dunmow in September 1943 when Boxted was allocated to the VIII Bomber Command, which expected to receive several new B-17 groups from the USA during the autumn and winter. However, a decision was taken to divert part of the heavy bomber force in training for the 8th Air Force to southern Italy to form the 15th Air Force and Boxted was one of three airfields in the Colchester area loaned to the 9th Air Force to house personnel from a number of fighter groups arriving in the UK. The first of these was the 354th Fighter Group at Greenham Common, which arrived at Boxted on 13 November. Colonel Kenneth R. Martin and his men discovered that not all accommodation was complete and some personnel made use of two farmhouses that had been taken over when the land was requisitioned. Langham Lodge, close to the technical site, was used by Group Headquarters staff. Meanwhile, the pilots, who had trained on P-39 Airacobras in the States, were receiving transition training to the new P-51B Mustang with the Packard-built Merlin

P-51B Mustangs of the 355th Fighter Squadron taking off from Boxted. (*USAF*)

Major James H. Howard being congratulated by Mr Robert M. Lovett, Assistant Secretary of War for Air, after receiving the Medal of Honor for his actions on 11 January 1944. (*USAF*)

engine. The 354th later adopted the name of 'The Pioneer Mustang Group'. Fighter Wings began to be activated by IX Fighter Command in November 1943. The 100th Fighter Wing was activated on 24 November under the command of Colonel David B. Lancaster at Boxted, moving its headquarters to Greenham Common on 6 December. The 70th Fighter Wing was assigned to IX Fighter Command on 6 December under command of Brigadier General James W. McCauley with its headquarters at Boxted.

On 1 December the 354th flew its first mission. Lieutenant Colonel 'Don' Blakeslee, Operations Officer of the 4th Fighter Group in the 8th Air Force who was assigned to help the new group enter combat, led them in a sweep over the Knocke area on the Belgian coast. Colonel Martin was flying on Lieutenant Colonel 'Don' Blakeslee's wing (Blakeslee was leading) as twenty-four Mustangs took off at 1429 hours and they flew an uneventful fighter sweep over Belgium and the Pas de Calais and landed at 1549 hours. The Group had flown its first combat sorties just twenty days after its first combat aircraft was assigned. For four months the 354th operated under the control of VIII Fighter Command, mainly on bomber support and escort. The first escort mission was flown on 5 December when Blakeslee led the Group to the Amiens area without incident. On the third Group mission on the 11th the Mustangs escorted the 1st Bomb Division Fortresses to Emden. Enemy fighters were seen but they evaded. On the 13th the Mustangs took the heavies 490 miles to Kiel, a new record for fighter escort. A Mustang was lost on this mission, but 1st Lieutenant (later Lieutenant Colonel) Glenn T. 'Eagle' Eagleston in the 353rd Fighter Squadron who caught a Bf 110, killed the rear gunner and knocked out the right engine to claim the first 'probable' for the Group. The first confirmed fighter kill for the new 9th and the 354th came on 16 December when the P-51s provided penetration support for the heavies at Bremen. 2nd Lieutenant Charles F. Gumm scored the kill. The same day, Major Owen M. Seaman, CO of the 353rd Squadron, was lost in the North Sea due to mechanical trouble. Four days later, while giving penetration support over Bremen and Wilhelmshaven, the 354th Fighter Group claimed 4-2-4 (destroyed-probably destroyed-damaged) for the loss of three P-51s. The Mustangs were nearly attacked by Thunderbolts whose pilots mistook them for Bf 109s. The month ended on the 31st with the tenth mission, over 500 miles to Bordeaux. By then the Group had claimed 8-3-6 aircraft for the loss of seven Mustangs.

On paper there were five fighter groups in 9th Fighter Command by January 1944 but only the 354th was operational. Its first January mission was flown on the 4th to Kiel. On the next day, when it also

Lieutenant Colonel James K. Howard (centre), CO of the 356th Fighter Squadron, with some fellow Mustang pilots at Boxted on 18 January 1944, just a week after flying the mission that resulted in his award of the Medal of Honor. (USAF)

Auxiliary fuel tanks being fitted to a P-51B 43-12451 GQ-I *Live Bait/'Peggy*. The plane was flown by 1st Lieutenant (later Captain) Clayton K. Gross from Walla Walla, Washington, in the 355th Fighter Squadron, 354th Fighter Group, in the winter of 1943-4. Clayton Gross finished the war with six confirmed victories. (*via Harry Holmes*)

gave target and withdrawal support to B-17s bombing Kiel, the 354th caught a gaggle of Bf 110s and single-engine fighters attacking the bombers and claimed 18-0-5 without loss. 1st Lieutenant (later Captain) Warren S. 'Red' Emerson in the 355th Fighter Squadron shot down one of the Bf 110s before it got to the Fortresses. Three minutes later he found more Bf 110s firing rockets at the bombers, attacked in a tight spiral and claimed a second enemy fighter before a rocket hit his Mustang and fragments cut his parachute harness and passed through his neck. Despite this and with his guns no longer firing he nevertheless attacked other Bf 110s, forcing them to break away from the bombers. Then, he flew the badly damaged P-51 back across the North Sea and landed safely, without brakes, in poor visibility. He was awarded a Bf 110 'destroyed' and one 'probably' destroyed. Emerson's final wartime score was six confirmed victories. Glenn T. 'Eagle' Eagleston scored his first victory on 5 January 1944 when he destroyed a FW 190 in the vicinity of Meldorf. By 13 April he had scored nine victories flying from Boxted.

Major (later Brigadier General) James H. Howard, CO of 356th Squadron, destroyed a total of 8.333 aircraft in World War 2, flying with the 2nd American Volunteer Group 'Flying Tigers' in China in 1942 and the 356th Fighter Squadron in the 354th Fighter Group in 1943-4. All six of his victories in the 354th Fighter Group, 20

December 1943 to 8 April 1944, were scored flying from Boxted. They included three in one day, 11 January 1944, when a maximum effort comprising all three 8th Air Force bomb divisions was mounted on aircraft factories at Waggum, Halberstadt and Oschersleben in the Brunswick area, a city notorious for its flak and fighter defences. (Altogether, the 354th accounted for 15-8-16 without loss, the largest contribution to the total of 28-13-24 claimed by all Groups.) Major James H. Howard displayed 'conspicuous gallantry and intrepidity above and beyond the call of duty' in action with the enemy near Oschersleben, when he came to the rescue of some Fortresses. Howard was flying his usual mount, *Ding Hao!* (Chinese for 'very good'). As the P-51s met the bombers in the target area numerous rocket-firing Bf 110 *Zerstören* attacked the bomber force. The 354th engaged and Howard destroyed one of the Bf 110s but in the fight lost contact with the rest of his Group. He immediately returned to the level of the bomber formation and saw that the B-17s of the 401st Bomb Group were being heavily attacked by German fighters and that no 'little friends' were on hand. Howard dived into the formation of more than thirty German fighters and for thirty minutes single-handedly pressed home a series of determined attacks. He shot down three fighters and probably destroyed and damaged others. Toward the end of his action, Howard continued to fight on with one remaining machine gun and his fuel supply dangerously low. Major Howard's brave single-handed action undoubtedly saved the formation. He was awarded the Medal of Honor.

In February 1944 the 354th met little opposition on its first four missions but for its fifth on 8 February after giving penetration, area and withdrawal support to the bombers in an attack on Frankfurt the 354th broke away and strafed targets of opportunity on the ground. Four P-51s and their pilots were lost and so for the time being no more ground strafing took place. On 10 February in the Brunswick area the 354th claimed 8-1-18 for the loss of three Mustangs and two pilots. The next day's mission was a bomber support at Frankfurt and the 354th claimed 14-0-10 against two aircraft lost. Colonel Martin got onto a Bf 110 and was closing for the kill when a Bf 109 which was chasing a Mustang flew across his path and the two aircraft collided. The Group CO baled out and was captured. Charles F. Gumm scored his fifth kill to become the first ace in the 9th Air Force and almost immediately, Lieutenant (later Lieutenant Colonel) Jack T. Bradley, Captain (later Lieutenant Colonel) Richard E. Turner and 1st

354th FG P-51B at Boxted. *(USAF)*

Lieutenant (later Captain) Don M. 'Buzz' Beerbower, a twenty-three-year-old pilot who was born in Saskatchewan, Canada, joined him. (By the end of March 1944 Beerbower had notched up a score of nine confirmed victories and seven damaged flying from Boxted. On 8 April he destroyed two FW 190s and a Bf 109 and damaged two more fighters to take his score to twelve.)

Lieutenant Colonel James H. Howard became Group CO on 12 February. That same month the 354th claimed 69-6-43½ while losing fourteen Mustangs and thirteen pilots. Many of these victories had been achieved during 'Big Week'. On the 20th the 354th claimed 16-2-6 without loss in the Leipzig area and the next day over Brunswick 10-2-7 were claimed against two aircraft lost. On the 22nd claims were 13-1-7 against one loss in the Oschersleben-Halberstadt area. Three days later the Group claimed 7-0-3 near Furth without loss and Charles F. Gumm scored his sixth confirmed kill to lead the Group. Gumm was killed on 1 March when his Mustang suffered an engine failure just after take-off from Boxted on a training flight. In March the 354th Group claimed thirty-seven aircraft destroyed.

In all, the 354th flew fifty-five combat missions from Boxted and forty-seven P-51s were lost in action. Claims were recorded for 169 enemy aircraft destroyed. The 353rd Fighter Squadron went on to score 290 air victories, a score unsurpassed by any other squadron in the USAAF. The Group had no fewer than thirty-nine aces by the end of the war. The top-scoring pilot was Glenn T. 'Eagle' Eagleston with 20.5 confirmed victories. Next highest scorer was Don 'Buzz' Beerbower with 15.5 victories. Captain Beerbower took command of the 353rd Fighter Squadron on 30 June 1944. His last victory was on

P-51s taking off from Boxted as B-17s pass overhead.

7 July. He was killed in action on 9 August 1944 when his Mustang was shot down by flak at Epernay airfield in the Reims area. The third highest scoring ace was Jack T. Bradley in the 353rd Fighter Squadron with fifteen confirmed victories, all except 5.5 of these while flying from Boxted. Next came Captain Kenneth H. Dahlberg in the 353rd Fighter Squadron, who scored all his fourteen victories from June to December 1944. Captain Dahlberg was shot down on 16 August 1944 but he successfully evaded only to be shot down again on 14 February 1945 when he was taken prisoner.

Next highest scoring ace was Wallace N. Emmer in the 353rd Fighter Squadron with fourteen confirmed victories. His first three victories were scored while flying from Boxted. On 9 August 1944 Captain Emmer was shot down while on patrol near Rouen and taken prisoner. He died of myocarditis in a PoW camp on 15 February 1945. Next was Major (later Colonel) Robert W. Stephens with thirteen victories, 7.5 kills being attributed to this pilot while flying from Boxed. Next came 1st Lieutenant (later Lieutenant Colonel) Lowell K. 'Brue' Brueland in the 355th Fighter Squadron with 12.5 confirmed victories. His first 3.5 confirmed victories were achieved flying from Boxted from 11 February to 9 April 1944. Colonel Brueland scored his thirteenth and fourteenth victories in Korea in 1953 when he destroyed two MiG-15s flying F-86 Sabres. Next came 1st Lieutenant, later Captain, Carl M. Frantz Junior in the 353rd Fighter Squadron with eleven confirmed victories, the first 5.5 kills being scored flying from Boxted. Also on eleven victories was Richard E. Turner in the 356th Fighter Squadron who scored eight of these victories flying from Boxted.The next highest scorer was 1st Lieutenant (later Colonel) Frank Q. 'Pinky' O'Connor with 10.75 victories, of which all except one were scored flying from Boxted in the 356th Fighter Squadron. Captain O'Connor was shot down and taken prisoner on 5 November 1944.

On 17 April 1944 the 354th moved to the advanced landing ground at Lashenden in Kent and the 56th Fighter Group, 8th Air Force, moved to Boxted; its P-47 Thunderbolts remaining until September 1945. The airfield was then transferred to the RAF on 23 October. A care and maintenance party remained until August 1947 when the last RAF personnel were withdrawn. During the late 1950s and early 1960s an agricultural spraying firm using Tiger Moths was based on the technical site. In 1963 the hangars and other buildings were auctioned off and the northern end was re-planted with apple orchards while the southern half was later used for arable farming. The runways and most of the other concrete were broken up by St Ives Sand and Gravel Company for road building. The barrack sites were bulldozed and graded to become the junction of the A12 and A120 on the Colchester northern bypass. A hotel was erected on a former barrack site adjacent to the old A12.

5

CHIPPING ONGAR
(Willingale)
(Station 162)

This airfield was constructed mostly in the parish of Willingale by US Army engineers who had planned to start in spring 1942 with completion by the end of the year but major work did not begin until August when the 831st Engineer Battalion (Aviation) arrived. They built three intersecting runways – the main of 6,000 feet and two of 4,200 feet – with a perimeter track with forty-eight loop hardstandings, two large loops and one pan. The underlying hardcore was largely

B-26 41-34968 *Lorellei* in the 387th Bomb Group under attack by flak guns in May 1944. (*USAF*))

Sequence of photos taken by the strike cameras on *Miss Ginger* in the 387th Bomb Group at 11,000 feet showing the demise of *King Bee* going down on the raid on Lille-Vendeville airfield on 31 August 1943 after it took a direct flak hit in the bomb bay. (*USAF*)

Colonel Jack E. Caldwell and *The Arkansas Traveler*, his personal Marauder while commanding the 387th Bomb Group at Chipping Ongar, which he took over on 8 November 1943. *The Arkansas Traveler* was lost with another crew a few weeks before Caldwell was killed on 13 April 1944. Instrumental in developing medium-level bombing tactics in the ETO, Caldwell was, in the words of one senior IX Bomber Command officer, 'a fine man'. (*USAF*)

B-26 Marauder in the 387th Bomb Group returning to Chipping Ongar after the raid on the marshalling yards at Amiens in September 1944. *(USAF)*

Blitz rubble from the East End of London. Two T2 hangars were erected and barracks to house 2,770 personnel were built on eight domestic sites in the surrounding countryside. Most of the main facilities were completed by the early spring of 1943 and the base was ready for occupation by June when the 387th Bomb Group arrived with its Marauders, which flew the North Atlantic ferry route from the US by way of Greenland and Prestwick.

They were the fourth Marauder group to arrive in Essex but raining was protracted and the Group did not fly their first combat mission until 15 August when crews joined the three other groups in an attack on St-Omer-Fort Rouge airfield. The Marauders made a long, straight bombing run and no fewer than eighteen B-26s were damaged by flak. Missions followed apace and on the afternoon of 25 August, twenty-one B-26s in the 387th Group attacked a power station at Rouen, dropping sixty-three 1,000-1b bombs on the objective. Enemy airfields in occupied countries were the main targets for the Marauders during the late summer of 1943, the 387th usually dispatching eighteen or thirty-six aircraft an each mission.

On 27 September a 387th Group B-26 flown by Lieutenant George Snyder was damaged by FW 190s. On fire in the fuselage and right engine, things looked bad for the Marauder, which dropped out of formation. Believing the ship to be doomed, one of the waist gunners baled out – and inadvertently dragged open the parachute of a second man, Staff Sergeant Laverne Stein, who was just behind. With his 'chute billowing from the waist hatch Stein lost his boots in the slipstream, which threatened to pull him out of the aircraft. Quick thinking by turret-gunner Sergeant Ed Kovalchik, who cut away the harness, saved Stein. In the meantime the fires had been extinguished, and Snyder had the Marauder under sufficient control to fly it back to England. Reaching Chipping Ongar, it was smoothly bellied in, the gear having refused to lower due to a loss of hydraulic pressure.

On 26 November when 198 Marauders were dispatched, Cambrai-Epinoy airfield was attacked by the 387th and 323rd Bomb Groups with 'negative' and 'good' results respectively. In the afternoon a V-weapon construction works at Audinghem in the Pas de Calais was bombed by the 323rd, 386th and 387th Bomb Groups with 'good to fair' results. Further raids on V-weapon sites were carried out during the winter of 1943–4 and the following spring. On 2 March 1944 when 353 IX Bomber Command Marauders hit V-weapons sites in Northern France for the morning mission, thirty-five B-26s of the 387th Bomb Group attacked the V-1 site at Linghem. The formation was led by a single aircraft from the 1st PFF Squadron. Three B-26s aborted with technical problems. The B-26s crossed into Belgium between Ostend and Nieuwpoort and were bracketed by flak. Aircraft in the first box bore the brunt of the flak. *Do It II* in the 559th Squadron was hit in the left engine and dropped away. The pilot, Lieutenant Lyster, nursed the

Chipping Ongar and the 558th Bomb Squadron, 387th Bomb Group, area photographed by an 8th Air Force Combat Cameraman in a B-17 from Watton in 1943. (*USAF*)

Chipping Ongar photographed by an 8th Air Force Combat Cameraman in a B-17 from Watton in 1943. *(USAF)*

B-26 out of the target area. *Hot Garters* had its right wing blown off after it was hit in the fuel tanks. Flight Officer Oliver Jopling, the pilot, could do nothing to save the aircraft but three men, including Jopling, survived when they managed to bale out of the doomed Marauder. So too did the bombardier, 1st Lieutenant Irving Lerman, but his parachute caught fire. The remaining aircraft, led by the pathfinder ship using *Oboe,* reached Linghem where bombing was described as 'poor to fair'. Typhoons of 1 and 3 Squadrons escorted the B-26s back to Earls Colne where they landed at 1230 hours. At around 1516 hours that afternoon the 387th dispatched thirty-nine aircraft and the 323rd thirty-six; these two groups forming up as a joint force for an attack on the Amiens-Longueau marshalling yards. The 387th Bomb Group's two boxes, of twenty-one (leading) and seventeen, went across the yards and bombed the tracks before avoiding overflying Glisy and instead arrowing out over the Somme in the direction of Arras, where the Marauders were picked up by their Spitfire IX escort over Le Treport. A total of 855 bombs had fallen on Longueau but many bombs overshot the long, curved track on the south side of the yards and twenty-four civilians were killed.

During eight months of operations under IX Bomber Command

from Chipping Ongar, the Group flew 204 missions, losing ten aircraft. On D-Day on 6 June 1944 the 387th Bomb Group was one of four B-26s groups in the assault by the IX Bomber Command formations upon three coastal batteries at Beau Guillot, La Madeleine and St-Martin de Varreville at *Utah* Beach. Two days later, when almost 400 B-26s hit fuel and ammunition dumps, railways, bridges and troop concentrations the 387th Bomb Group flew a successful morning mission that hit the rail junction at Pontaubault. Captain Robert E. Will's flight carried out the best bombing, Lieutenant Rudolf Tell his bombardier placing the bombs exactly on target. In the afternoon, Captain Rollin D. Childress was briefed to lead eighteen Marauders to knock out a fuel dump in the Fôret de Grimbosq south of Caen. Take-off was at 1958 hours, and, although the ceiling was at 900 feet, the formation assembled without difficulty. *En route* and climbing through the overcast, the B-26s became dispersed and eleven Marauders returned to base. One had to crash-land at Gravesend in Kent and a second B-26 piloted by 1st Lieutenant Raymond V. Morin crashed while landing at Friston, Suffolk. Childress meanwhile, gathered up three aircraft and pressed on. The flight dropped to deck level at times, the pilots trying to pick up landmarks in terrible visibility, which was down to a quarter of a mile in places. Finally picking up the target, Childress made his run and bombed from 6,000 feet, guided by his bombardier, 1st Lieutenant Wilson J. Cushing. As the Marauders turned away, buffeted from the resulting explosions, the crews knew that the dump had been destroyed. Then they were enveloped in flak, moderate at first and then heavy with alarming accuracy. The B-26 flown by Captain Charles W. Shrober exploded in mid-air and no 'chutes were seen to emerge from the stricken aircraft. Among the dead was Captain John D. Root, the 387th Weather Officer. Heading for home, the three B-26s plunged through the weather to make a landfall over England. They put down at Chipping Ongar at 2230 hours. Group CO Colonel Thomas M. Seymour offered his congratulations on the tenacity displayed by Childress – a view endorsed by the 98th Wing commander, Colonel Millard Lewis. Later a telegram arrived from the army, stating that the bombing had destroyed enough fuel for an entire *Panzer* division.

The 387th Bomb Group's last mission from the base, on 18 July, was just prior to moving to Stoney Cross, in the New Forest, the rear party leaving on the 21st. After the 387th had vacated the station, only a USAAF station complement party remained and control passed from

Men of the 831st Engineer Battalion (Aviation) at work at Chipping Ongar on 11 January 1943. (USAF)

the 9th Air Force to the USSTAF. The base was then allocated to the Air Disarmament Command preparing, as its name suggests, for the task of taking over captured *Luftwaffe* installations and equipment. The numbers of personnel of the constituent units involved was not great and the base was under-utilised. A few transport and light communications aircraft were occasionally on the airfield, but there was comparatively little flying. This organisation relinquished the airfield in January 1945.

During September 1944, Chipping Ongar was used temporarily by IX Troop Carrier Command as an advanced base for Operation *Market* but a planned glider mission was cancelled on the 26th. In mid-March 1945, the C-47s of the 61st Troop Carrier Group arrived to carry paratroops of the British 6th Airborne Division to Wesel during Operation *Varsity* on the 24th. Of the eighty aircraft despatched, one Pathfinder C-47 was lost. After the mission the aircraft returned directly to their home base in France.

Chipping Ongar airfield had been officially returned to the RAF on

1 March and on 18 April it was placed under the control of Bomber Command. On 11 June that year it was transferred to Technical Training Command as a satellite of Hornchurch with a small RAF holding party. There were various paper transfers during the post-war period but in October 1948 the RAF staff withdrew and a civilian warden watched over the deserted sites for Reserve Command. The local farmers were given tenancies for cultivation of land between the runways, and on 28 February 1959 the airfield was officially relinquished and returned to the original owners. In the mid-1960s the runways and concrete were broken up by the St Ives Sand and Gravel Company for use as hard core, much being used for the Brentwood bypass section of the A12.

6

EARLS COLNE

(Station 358)

The Marks Hall estate was the site of the first heavy bomber airfield built in Essex. Work began early in January 1942 and by September, when an RAF holding party moved in, the runways, perimeter track and most hardstandings had been completed by the main contractor, W. & C. French Limited. The flying field was to current Class A standard with a 6,000 feet main runway and two of 4,200 feet. Like other airfields of the same period, it was originally laid out with thirty-six pan-type hardstandings but, after Earls Colne was allocated for USAAF use on 4 June 1942, an additional sixteen loop hardstandings were added, one pan being eliminated in the process. Two T2 hangars and technical site buildings were erected and barracks' accommodation for 2,570 personnel was built on seven dispersed domestic sites.

Flying through flak the 455th Bomb Squadron, 323rd Bomb Group, runs in to the target at Dieppe. The flak bursts killed the bombardier of the aircraft at far right, although it still dropped its bombs. (*USAF*)

Sergeant William F. Vermillion (left) and navigator Lieutenant Ralph N. Phillips (with seven mission bombs painted on his M1 steel helmet, both of which have a 'flying Eightball' emblem) wearing M1 flak vests over the M3 apron, in the 455th Bomb Squadron, 323rd Bomb Group, at Earls Colne in 1944 beside B-26C 41-34692 *Mr Fala* named after President Roosevelt's dog. Phillips was the first B-26 crewman to complete fifty combat missions in the ETO. (*USAF*)

A B-26 in the 453rd Bomb Squadron, 323rd Bomb Group, with its left engine on fire during the attack on Wittlich in 1944. (USAF)

The first US organisation to arrive was a 600-man-strong service unit in October 1942 but it only stayed a few weeks. The first aircraft to land at the airfield is believed to have been B-17F 41-24352 *Holy Joe* in the 352nd Bomb Squadron, 301st Bomb Group, at Chelveston, when it made an emergency landing on 9 October 1942 returning from the mission to Lille. Three wounded crew members were removed from the Fortress and taken to hospital. Apart from temporary use by F-5 Lightning photographic aircraft as a forward base and emergency landings by a variety of types returning from operations, Earls Colne remained vacant until May 1943 when the 94th Bomb Group (Heavy), arrived. This Group's stay was brief for in June the 8th Air Force moved its B-17s to Suffolk in an exchange of bases with B-26 groups and the 323rd Bomb Group commanded by Colonel Herbert B. Thatcher and his B-26 Marauder crews took over.

Medium-altitude bombing missions by B-26s from the UK began on 16 July 1943 when the 323rd Bomb Group dispatched sixteen Marauders to the marshalling yards at Abbeville. They took off at around 1800 hours and climbed to rendezvous with their Spitfire escort at 10,000 feet. Fourteen Marauders bombed the target, two men were wounded by flak and ten aircraft were damaged, but none was lost. The Group's second mission was to the coke ovens at Ghent on 25 July when eighteen B-26s were dispatched. Six aircraft were damaged by flak but there were no crew casualties. The 323rd's third mission was on the morning of the 26th but only fifteen out of the eighteen aircraft that were dispatched managed to locate and bomb St-Omer-Fort

Crews of the famous Dam Busters of 617 Squadron RAF, including Flight Lieutenant Joe McCarthy, an American (fourth from right), pose beside B-26B 41-17750 and crew in the 452nd Bomb Squadron, 323rd Bomb Group, on 18 August 1943. *(USAF)*

Rouge airfield, the briefed target. Two days later 119 P-47 Thunderbolts escorted seventeen B-26s in the 323rd Bomb Group on the raid on Triqueville airfield. On the 28th the 323rd Bomb Group sent seventeen B-26s to bomb the coke ovens at Zeebrugge. A second mission later that day by eighteen Marauders to Triqueville had to be aborted when the Marauders failed to rendezvous with the P-47 escort.

During the morning of 29 July eighteen B-26s in the 323rd Bomb Group set out to bomb Amsterdam-Schiphol but they brought their bombs back when the target was found to be cloud-covered. Late in the afternoon more B-26s headed for the airfield at St-Omer-Fort Rouge which was successfully bombed. Flak damaged eight aircraft. Four separate missions were flown by the Marauders on 31 July – the largest-scale effort to date. The 323rd Bomb Group flew two missions in the morning with eighteen Marauders attacking Merville airfield and nineteen Poix/Nord to drop a total of 44 tons of bombs. One B-26 from the force attacking Poix was lost along with its seven-man crew, and seven other aircraft sustained flak damage. On 2 August forty-nine

Marauders in the 323rd and 386th Bomb Groups were sent to Merville and St-Omer-Fort Rouge airfields respectively. Flak put holes in twenty-eight of the bombers; one B-26 was so badly damaged that it had to make a forced landing in England. Six crewmen were wounded.

In 1943 Captain John R. 'Tex' McCrary, an experienced journalist and war reporter, visited Earls Colne and wrote a fine piece about the 323rd Bomb Group.

> One of the boys who rides the Marauders has linked the Jap and German fronts with his story – Captain Fred Kappeler from Alameda, California. He's the Group Navigator for Colonel Thatcher's outfit. Before he came here, he was in one of the Mitchells that followed Doolittle to Tokyo...He went on up into China after that job, and fought with Chennault's outfit for a while. The most B-25s we ever got in the air at one time was about 15. And then he got serious, very serious: 'You know the kind of a job I'd like to get? I'd like to get a job planning deals like Ploesti and Tokyo. The kind of jobs that just can't be done, but we figure out a way to do them. You know the best way to

Yellow-nosed B-26B 42-96165, which was known as the *Big Hairy Bird* in the 599th Bomb Squadron, 397th Bomb Group, with shark teeth. When the aircraft was later transferred to the 558th Bomb Squadron, 387th Bomb Group, shortly before the end of the war a 'tiger tail' stripe was added. (*USAF*)

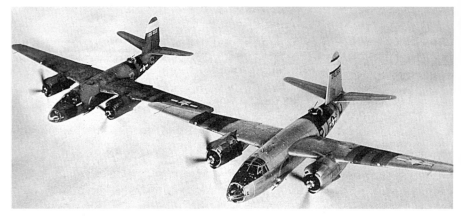

Two B-26 Marauders in the 454th Bomb Squadron, 323rd Bomb Group, in formation. (*USAF*)

Back with *Bingo Buster* in the 454th Bomb Squadron, 323rd Bomb Group, the second UK-based Marauder to complete 100 missions, pilot 1st Lieutenant Robert Lind 'mits' crew chief Wendell Polonski while the rest of the crew look on. *Bingo Buster* then had a total of 466 hours 40 minutes flying time, one of her original engines and a record of never having a crew member wounded. The ordnance used is M38 practice bombs. (*USAF*)

Marauders in the 598th Bomb Squadron, 397th Bomb Group, in formation. *(USAF)*

get a job done in the Air Forces? Just tell the boys it's dangerous and act like you don't think they can pull it off. That's all you got to do... That's sort of the way the Marauders got started, too. And it must be the right way. Today they've become the foundation of the whole 9th Air Force.

On 19 October 1943 the 323rd Bomb Group was transferred from the 8th to the 9th Air Force. Operations continued as before with the same target range, although from December the Group was frequently despatched to so-called *Noball* targets in the Pas de Calais. These were then identified as possible installations for launching rockets at

A B-26 Marauder passing Earls Colne airfield. Marks Hall, the 9th Air Force HQ south-west of the airfield, is at the top centre of the photo in the wooded area. The Hall was demolished shortly after the end of the war. (USAF)

England. On 13 November Colonel Wilson R. Wood took over command from Colonel Thatcher and the 323rd Bomb Group soon became known as 'Wood's Rocket Raiders'. As spring approached, more attacks were directed at marshalling yards and other communication targets and fewer missions were run to the *Noballs*.

On 2 March when 353 IX Bomber Command Marauders hit V-weapons sites in Northern France for the morning mission the 323rd Bomb Group dispatched fifty-four Marauders, divided into three boxes, to Tournehem and Lostebarne, south of Ardes, in the Fôret Nationale de Tournehem, north-west of Lumbres. The Marauders had two Typhoon squadrons as escort. The 323rd's visual bombing of Tournehem was 'good' but the attack on the site at Lostebarne was only rated as 'poor'. To test the mobility of the Group, there was a quick change of base with the 386th Bomb Group on 22 March. While the 322nd Bomb Group's B-26s were at Earls Colne a Ju 88, shot down by an RAF night fighter, crashed on top of and destroyed a B-26. Two of the *Luftwaffe* crew were killed in the incident but two others had earlier parachuted safely.

In mid-May the 323rd Bomb Group was sent against rail bridges for the first time and these featured regularly in the weeks prior to D-Day.

On 16 May B-26C *Bingo Buster* in the 454th Bomb Squadron became the first in the 323rd Bomb Group to complete 100 missions and only the second Marauder in the ETO to do so. Like *Mild and Bitter* this aircraft was rotated home to show the flag for AAF recruiting. On 20 May the 323rd Bomb Group despatched thirty-five aircraft to targets in the Dieppe dock area under Spitfire escort. During the attack a B-26B in the 453rd Bomb Squadron flown by Major J. Heather was hit by two flak bursts and was last seen going down in the target area. A second Marauder was hit by a heavy burst, as was a B-26B in the 454th

B-26s in the 454th Bomb Squadron, 323rd Bomb Group, dropping their bombs on a target on the continent. (*USAF*)

Squadron, which fell out of formation and exploded in mid-air near Calais.

On D-Day, the 323rd Bomb Group flew three eighteen-plane formations instead of the usual thirty-six to bomb targets near the beachhead. On 13 June General George Marshall, chief of the US Army and General 'Hap' Arnold, chief of the US Army Air Forces, made a short visit to Earls Colne. On 11 July the 323rd Bomb Group began leaving for Beaulieu airfield on the fringe of the New Forest in Hampshire and by 21 July sixty Marauders had all left. Earls Colne was little used for several weeks and in September was taken over by RAF 38 Group and the Albemarles and Halifaxes of 296 and 297 Squadrons. These took part in the airborne operations in the Low Countries and the Rhine crossing in March 1945. After the war the airfield was placed on a care and maintenance basis until finally, in 1965, a large part of the airfield was purchased from an investment company by Eric Hobbs, who initially farmed all the available land. St Ives Sand and Gravel broke up the runways for aggregate, which was used to improve the A12 from September 1965 to February 1967. The hangar on the technical site was let for storage and Mr Hobbs converted buildings or constructed others for light engineering, the whole of the former technical site becoming an industrial area. In 1990, Eric Hobbs converted the airfield into two eighteen-hole golf courses and he added a clubhouse, restaurant and leisure facilities.

7

GOSFIELD
(Station 154)

On 18 August 1942 the 816th Engineer Battalion (Aviation) began setting up tented accommodation at Gosfield to begin construction of an airfield. A shortage of construction equipment and other problems delayed work in the early months and autumn rains often turned the underlying clay into mud. Little progress was made and early in March 1943 most of the 816th personnel were transferred to the more advanced site at Great Saling. Full-scale construction at Gosfield was only resumed in August. By mid-October three runways, one 6,000 feet long and two others, 4,200 feet and 4,000 feet long, and fifty-one hardstandings and two T2 hangars had been constructed. The 833rd Engineer Battalion then took over to begin construction of eight domestic sites for 3,278 personnel and other facilities to the south-west of the airfield. On the night of 11 December Dornier 217s dropped a

A-20J or K lead ship in the 410th Bomb Group with flash suppressors on the turret guns and underwing bomb-racks for an additional 1,000 lb of bombs. (USAF)

A-20G/H gun-nosed Havocs in the 646th Squadron, 410th Bomb Group, with a J/K bombardier ship in the lead position. *(USAF)*

number of bombs, some of which fell on occupied buildings at Gosfield, killing eight US personnel, wounding seven seriously and twenty-one slightly.

Personnel in the 365th Fighter Group began arriving at Gosfield on 23 December 1943 after a rail journey from Scotland to Halstead to begin training on P-47s under the command of Colonel Lance Call. It was some weeks before the full complement of seventy-five P-47D Thunderbolts arrived and mid-February before the Group was operational. The first mission was flown on 22 February when the P-47s flew a bomber support sweep over enemy-held territory. Early missions were in support of bomber operations and on one of these on 2 March, the 365th had its first encounter with enemy fighters (JG 26) in the Bastogne area, resulting in the loss of one Thunderbolt and claims of six of the enemy shot down. They included three FW 190A-6/7s in the 6th *Staffel*. Two of the German pilots, including *Leutnant* Friedrich Lange, the *Staffelkapitän*, were killed and the third was WIA (wounded in action). *Oberstleutnant* Egon Mayer the JG 2 *Kommodore*, who was flying his 353rd sortie, was also shot down at

Montmédy by a Thunderbolt in the 365th Fighter Group and was killed. Mayer's total score was 102 victories, which included twenty-five four-engined bombers. It was on this day that Major (later Colonel) Robert L. Coffey Junior claimed the first of his six confirmed victories of the war when he shot down a FW 190 west of Luxemburg. Three days later, with only nine combat missions flown, the 365th Fighter Group moved south to Beaulieu in Hampshire. During their short stay at Gosfield two P-47s were missing in action and two pilots had been killed in local flying accidents.

Early in April, Marauders of the 397th Bomb Group, the last of eleven medium- and light-bomber groups to join the 9th Air Force in England, began arriving at Gosfield after a transatlantic crossing by the southern route via Africa. The Group, which was commanded by Colonel Richard T. Coiner Junior and which was composed of the 596th, 597th, 598th and 599th Squadrons, became part of the 98th CBW (Combat Bombardment Wing). On 8 April administrative control of the 97th, 98th and 99th Wings passed to the direct control of IX Bomber Command. No sooner had the 397th Bomb Group arrived than they were moved to Rivenhall on 14 April when that airfield was vacated by the 363rd Tactical Reconnaissance Group. The following

A 645th Bomb Squadron A-20J or K over occupied Europe. (USAF)

A-20G _Zombia_ in the 645th Bomb Squadron, 410th Bomb Group, lies wrecked in a field having completed 101 missions. _(Merle Olmsted Coll)_

day, personnel of the 410th Bomb Group (L), which was equipped with A-20 Havocs, arrived from Birch. The 410th was commanded by Colonel Ralph Rhudy and comprised the 644th, 645th, 646th and 647th Bomb Squadrons. In the US the 410th had been trained in low-level attack and crews expected this type of mission in the ETO but once the A-20s had been received from depots the Group commenced a hurried theatre conversion to medium-altitude bombing before it could make its combat debut.

The 410th Bomb Group (L) flew its first mission on 1 May when some of its crews flew in aircraft of the 416th Group. The target was a V-1 site north of Le Havre, just in from the French coast. The box leader made two passes and bombs were scattered all over the area, from the IP (Initial Point) to the target. Some crews failed to find anything worthwhile to drop on, and brought their bombs back. It was said that the bombardiers lacked full confidence in handling the Norden bombsight and while there was gradual improvement, on only

A-20J _Maxine_ in the 410th Bomb Group with the state map of Texas below the cockpit. _(USAF)_

A-20 Havoc *Angel II* in the 645th Bomb Squadron, 410th Bomb Group, at Gosfield. L–R: Chester Dunaj, Earl Bever and Fred Yoos. Kneeling is William Dorward the ground crew chief. Dunaj, Bever and Yoos were lost on the mission to Brest in September 1944. (USAF)

two missions during May and one in June was the bombing officially rated as 'excellent'. Eventually, there were sixty-four Havocs at Gosfield, sixteen per squadron, all in camouflage finish, and missions followed thick and fast, often two per day. Targets were airfields, railways, bridges, fuel and military stores, V-weapon sites, road junctions and enemy troop positions. On 4 May the A-20s of the 410th Bomb Group (L) joined other Havocs and Marauders in bombing industrial targets and marshalling yards for the first time. While at Gosfield the 410th flew twenty-six pre-D-Day missions. During twenty weeks of operations from Gosfield the 410th flew 124 missions, losing twenty A-20s, almost all to flak.

On the mission to the Amiens marshalling yards on 27 May 1944 the 410th dispatched thirty-eight A-20G and five A-20J aircraft in two boxes. They arrived over Amiens early and attempted to carry out the

A-20G/H 6Q-V in the 647th Bomb Squadron, 410th Bomb Group.
(USAF)

A-20 43-10195 8U-U Queen Julia in the 646th Bomb Squadron. *(USAF)*

A-20 43-21745 8U-S The Real McCoy in the 646th Bomb Squadron. *(USAF)*

mission as briefed. Crossing the town and with the marshalling yards in their sights, both boxes released their loads. The lead box of the first wave dropped roughly in the right place, if a little short – but all the following boxes, in both attacks, scattered bombs not on the marshalling yard but across the built-up areas of Amiens, wrecking many houses and causing inevitable casualties. Few if any bombs from the following boxes fell where they were intended. One A-20G in the 647th Bomb Squadron, flown by Lieutenant Richard K. Robinson, was shot down by flak. That same evening the 410th and the two other A-20 Groups returned to Amiens. At 2105 hours two boxes of Havocs for their bombs away. The A-20G-35 piloted by 2nd Lieutenant Warren A. Thompson in the 647th Bomb Squadron was hit by flak and fire took hold in the left engine nacelle. The Havoc dropped out of formation but the crew was lucky to abandon the aircraft in good order, all members coming down not far from a flak battery at Bray-sur-Somme.

On 3 June the Havocs of the 410th Bomb Group took off on their thirty-second Group mission of the war when more than 250 aircraft

A-20s in the 410th Bomb Group bombing an enemy target. (*USAF*)

A-20G/H *Dear Mom.* (*USAF*)

A-20J *Li'l Suzie* in the 410th Bomb Group. (*USAF*)

A-20J *Irene* in the 410th Bomb Group on 22 June 1944. (*USAF*)

A-20 8U-S in the 646th Bomb Squadron. *(USAF)*

set out to attack airfields, coastal gun batteries and road bridges in northern France. One A-20 in the 644th Bomb Squadron, whose primary target was Chartres airfield, was hit by flak. With its centre fuselage wrapped in flames Lieutenant Benjamin D. Randolph struggled to keep the A-20 in the air but his efforts were to no avail and the aircraft fell away, taking Randolph and his crew, Staff Sergeants David A. Sagag and Frank Desanno, to their deaths. A fine pilot, popular with everyone, Ben Randolph had been an original member of the squadron during its training days in the US. His loss was deeply felt.

On 3 July 1944 Colonel Sherman R. Beaty took command of the 410th from Colonel Ralph Rhudy. Following the Allied break-out from the Normandy beachhead in late July and the subsequent sweep across France, the 410th, in common with other IX Bomber Command units, found range was a critical factor. To remedy this situation, the expected move to France was finally ordered for 18 September when the majority of personnel were moved by train to Southampton for the sea crossing and onward journey to A-58 at Coulommiers.

A-20s in the 410th Bomb Group. *(USAF)*

This was the end of the 9th Air Force tenure at Gosfield but the airfield remained under USAAF control with a small station complement to deal with the occasional forced landing and visitor. In January 1945 299 Squadron RAF arrived from Wethersfield for two weeks with Stirlings but soon left for Shepherds Grove. In mid-March the airfield was one of a number of bases in Essex that was used by the First Allied Airborne Army during the crossing of the Rhine and 271, 512 and 575 Squadrons RAF arrived from Broadwell with Dakotas and Horsas. These flew out on 24 March, the aircraft returning to their home stations after the *Varsity* operation. Gosfield was then used as a collecting point for recovered Horsa gliders. After being put into an RAF care and maintenance unit much of the airfield was returned to agricultural use and the hangars and other buildings were auctioned off in 1955. In the late 1980s the runways and perimeter track were broken up by St Ives Sand and Gravel for hard core. Some of the remaining buildings were taken over by light engineering and plant hire companies.

GREAT DUNMOW
(Little Easton)
(Station 164)

This airfield was constructed on the Easton Lodge estate, which was owned by the Countess of Warwick and her granddaughter Mrs Felice Spurrier, by the US 818th Engineer Battalion (Aviation), which began laying the ground work in the late summer of 1942. Much of the site was ancient parkland and over 200 mature trees had to be removed. The base was scheduled for completion by the following March but by then only the three runways (the main one 6,000 feet long and the other two both 4,200 feet long) and the perimeter track had been laid. Later, fifty loop hardstands were added. The base was finally ready for operational use on 1 July 1943, although many facilities had yet to be completed. Two T2 hangars and a blister were eventually provided and the domestic accommodation on seven sites to the north of the airfield eventually housed 2,888 personnel.

B-26B-45-MA 42-95808 O8-C *Idiot's Delight* in the 575th Bomb Squadron, 391st Bomb Group. *(USAF)*

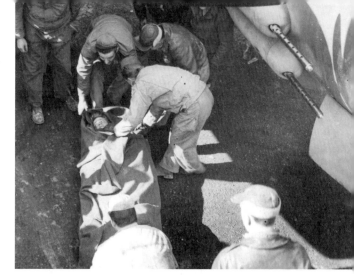

A wounded crewmember is rushed to hospital *(USAF)*

B-26 41-31877 RU-V *Bar Fly* in the 554th Bomb Squadron, 386th Bomb Group, at Great Dunmow was a long-serving veteran in the ETO. On 9 May 1944 it was the first B-26 to complete 100 missions, only to crash in the US during a bond tour. *(USAF)*

Men, mouth and guns! *(USAF)*

A B-26 of the 386th Bomb Group that crashed at Great Dunmow being sprayed with foam. (*USAF*)

During late September the 386th Bomb Group and its Marauders arrived from Boxted after that base had been allocated to the 4th Wing. Great Dunmow was considered only half complete. The 386th, which was commanded by Colonel Lester J. Maitland, was now assigned to the 3rd Wing. On 2 September 104 B-26s dropped just short of 150 tons of bombs on fuel dumps and airfields located in the Rouen-Hesdin-Lille areas. The 386th and 387th Groups each split their strength into two to attack targets simultaneously but dense cloud cover prevented the 387th from bombing. The 386th's thirty-six aircraft (less one) did, however, manage to unload over Mazingarbe, with fair results. In return for its disappointing effort, the 387th lost an aircraft and had thirteen damaged. Five men were wounded and six were MIA (missing in action). On 7 September confusion over the rendezvous point resulted in the 386th Group abandoning any attempt to reach the marshalling yards at Lille, while only a third of the 387th's thirty-six Marauders managed to attack the yards at St Pol-sur-Mer.

On 3 October an ambitious, multiple-airfield strike involving 252 aircraft from all four 3rd Wing groups, attacked Lille, Schiphol, Woensdrecht, Haamstede and Beauvais aerodromes. The 386th and 387th Groups bombed Beauvais as well as the Dutch airfields. One of

The crew of *Loretta Young* in the 553rd Bomb Squadron, 386th Bomb Group, at Great Dunmow. The actress had autographed the nose of Lieutenant 'Moe' Elling's B-26 before the crew left the USA for England. *(USAF)*

the 386th's aircraft was so badly damaged that it had to be written off on return and no fewer than seventy-four B-26s suffered varying degrees of battle damage, although there were no crew casualties. On 16 October the 386th and the other 3rd Wing groups were re-assigned to the 9th Air Force. The 386th Bomb Group had flown twenty-eight combat missions when it arrived and over the course of the next twelve months flew another 257.

On 29 November when the B-26 groups attacked Chièvres airfield, *Sexation*, a 553rd Bomb Squadron Marauder piloted by Captain Irving T. 'Pete' LaFramboise, ran through a deadly concentration of flak which destroyed the hydraulic system, damaged the right engine and so crippled the Marauder that it fell out of formation. As soon as it was beyond the protection of the squadron formation, *Sexation* was set upon by six enemy fighters. In their first pass, the fighters shattered the top turret, disabled the rudder and wounded the waist gunner. The tail gunner, Staff Sergeant William H. Norris, one of his two guns disabled

General Dwight D. Eisenhower's tour of airfields on 11 April included a visit to Great Dunmow. Here, strike photos are shown to General Eisenhower in the operations building. L–R: General Lewis H. Brereton, Commander 9th Air Force; Lieutenant General Sherman Beaty, 386th Bomb Group Executive Officer; Eisenhower; Colonel Herbert B. Thatcher CO, 99th Bomb Wing, which was also based at Great Dunmow. (*USAF*)

On 23 June 1944 *Blazing Heat* in the 386th Bomb Group suffered a nose-over at Great Dunmow. The aircraft had flown over ninety missions and this saved it from the scrap heap. (*USAF*)

Douglas A-26C Invader in the 553rd Bomb Squadron, 386th Bomb Group, at Great Dunmow. *(USAF)*

by the flak, shot a German fighter down as it came in. In 1940 Bill Norris and Irving LaFramboise had been aerialists with Wallace Brothers Circus in the Chicago area. In 1942 LaFramboise and Norris met on the street in Tampa, Florida. They discovered that they were both assigned to the 386th but in different squadrons. They completed their training in the same crew and went to England.

Sexation's top turret gunner could only fire blindly from his shattered turret and the B-26 was damaged again by the fighters. The Marauder went into several uncontrolled but brief dives. Norris was thrown violently from his position into the waist where he recovered, manned the waist guns and fought off two more fighter passes. Then he returned to his tail turret, shot down a second enemy fighter and, alternately firing waist and tail guns, kept the remaining fighters from getting too close until fighter escort was reached. The fighter attacks, however, had further critically damaged the Marauder, putting the left

B-26 Marauder *The Mad Russian* in the 386th Bomb Group pictured at Ridgewell on 27 November 1943. This aircraft was flown by Lieutenant Danny Klimovich. *(USAF)*

B-26 *We'll Be There* in the 555th Bomb Squadron at Great Dunmow in August 1943. *(USAF)*

engine out of action and destroying the compass and other instruments. Despite all the damage and being kept in the air by only one damaged engine, LaFramboise and his co-pilot Robert Beckhoff flew the B-26 back across the English Channel. Unnecessary equipment was thrown overboard and they managed to get *Sexation* to RAF Manston in Kent where LaFramboise made a smooth crash-landing, although the landing gear was jammed and the bomb bay doors open. Captain 'Pete' LaFramboise and Bill Norris, the two former aerialists, were awarded the Silver Star.

On 22 January 1944 Colonel Joe Kelly took over command of the 386th Bomb Group from Colonel Richard C. Sanders. On 2 March 1944 when 353 IX Bomber Command Marauders hit V-weapons sites in Northern France for the morning mission the 386th Bomb Group dispatched fifty-four B-26s divided into three boxes for an attack on the *Noball* site at Losterbarne, Tournehem and Lottinghem, north of

B-26 *Bomb Boogie* in the 553rd Bomb Squadron at Great Dunmow in August 1943. *(USAF)*

B-26 *Our Baby* in the 553rd Bomb Squadron at Great Dunmow in August 1943. *(USAF)*

B-26 4-F at Great Dunmow on 25 February 1944. *(USAF)*

Fruges. *Oboe* was used to assist navigation and confirm target location. *En route*, one crew aborted the mission with a malfunction and returned to Great Dunmow. One of the two spare aircraft replaced it in the formation. At 0929 hours the 386th rendezvoused with their escort of Typhoon Ibs of 181 and 245 Squadrons and nine minutes later crossed the coast south of Le Touquet heading for the IP at Fruges. The objective was picked up visually at 0945 hours. In their distinctive arrowhead flights, the 386th had no problem forming up into three separate attack waves and the leading box of eighteen B-26s headed for the site at Lostebarne, the second (seventeen aircraft) aiming for the target in the trees of the forest at Tournehem and the third (also seventeen aircraft) going to Lottinghem. Bombs were away at 0949 hours. Crews saw evidence of excavations around the Lostebarne site as well as one of the familiar ski-shaped buildings used for storage of flying bombs. The second wave had bombed the V-1 site at Tournehem with good results. The third wave encountered overcast and completely missed the site at Lottinghem, all bombs falling to the north-east. A total of 102 500-lb GP bombs were dropped, the results by the lead and low flights being rated as 'good', although thirty of the bombs dropped by the low flight fell south-west of the target. Adopting a dog-leg flight path out of the target area, the 386th crossed the coast between Calais

B-26 *Sexy Betsy* in the 555th Bomb Squadron at Great Dunmow in August 1943. *(USAF)*

and Dunkirk and arrived back over Great Dunmow at 1035 hours.

During the afternoon five boxes totalling ninety-one B-26s (fifty-three from the 322nd Bomb Group and thirty-eight from the 386th) went to the marshalling yards at Tergnier escorted by four Typhoon squadrons, with three more as back-up. Tergnier was an important rail junction as it carried traffic serving Paris and numerous points throughout north-western France. It also contained extensive locomotive-repair facilities. Take-off for the bombers was at 1455 hours. The 322nd made up the lead boxes with the 386th following. Two B-26s in the 322nd formation returned early with mechanical problems before the rest crossed the French coast at Le Treport at 1615 hours. The Marauders encountered heavy cloud which confused the bombardiers, who identified not Tergnier but the town of St Quentin, about thirteen miles to the north. There was considerable confusion as the lead flights made a right turn away from the real target and headed for St Quentin. All fifty-one of the 322nd's Marauders passed the IP over Roye. They picked up some ineffectual flak from batteries at Montdidier, but there were no reported incidents as a result. The bombers ploughed on and some released their loads at 1659 hours.

Only twenty-three crews bombed but the 184 500-pounders killed sixty-five people in the town and damaged 300 dwellings. Meanwhile, the 386th had correctly located Tergnier where the thirty-eight B-26s of the 386th bombed the rail yard, while four boxes (nineteen aircraft) attacked the (secondary) *Luftwaffe* airfield at Rosières-en-Santerre. A number of enemy aircraft were observed by the crews as their bombs were released, the bursts appearing to be right on target. The raid was judged to have achieved excellent results, with a number of buildings and dispersal areas having received direct hits. Four more boxes of the 386th bombed the airfield at Amiens/Glisy where all the bombs exploded on the runways and the dispersal areas.

On 11 April General Eisenhower, Major General Carl Spaatz and Major General Lewis Brereton visited Great Dunmow to watch the 386th Bomb Group mission take-off. Lord Trenchard, the 'father of the RAF' and Air Chief Marshal Sir Trafford Leigh-Mallory also visited the base. So too did Cornelius Ryan, a *Daily Telegraph* correspondent who later wrote *The Longest Day* and *A Bridge Too Far*. Ryan also hitched a ride with one of the 386th Bomb Group crews on D-Day.

In July 1944 the 553rd Bomb Squadron Operations Officer Captain

B-26 *Rat poison* in the 553rd Bomb Squadron at Great Dunmow with ground crew in August 1943. *(USAF)*

B-26 *The Mad Russian* in the 555th Bomb Squadron with ground crew at Great Dunmow in August 1943. *(USAF)*

Lee R. Meyers and Group Operations Officer Lieutenant Colonel Harry G. 'Tad' Hankey were greatly surprised to receive the first of eighteen A-26B/glass-nosed A-26C Invaders at Great Dunmow from Prestwick for initial combat evaluation. General Anderson briefed Hankey that he would be taking charge of the group of crews bringing Invaders in from the States and would lead the first five missions on the new aircraft. The Colonel in charge of the group from the US was convinced that the A-26 could bomb at medium altitude and then go down to strafe, something that Marauder veterans knew was highly questionable. The first A-26 to arrive at Great Dunmow landed and slid off the end of the runway and another stalled halfway down the runway and came to rest at right-angles to it. A third A-26, which hit the stalled aircraft with his left wing, also ended up in the mud. In all, six Invaders were damaged and only those pilots who had made a good landing were allowed to check out as pilots in the 553rd, while the rest became co-pilots on the B-26s. One A-26B had crashed fatally at Great Dunmow in August during a brief demonstration flight for the benefit of 2 Group RAF who were considering operating the Invader in British service to replace the Boston and possibly the Mitchell. Eight A-26 missions were flown during the evaluation by the 553rd Squadron, between 6 September (when an attack on German strongpoints at Brest was attempted) and 19 September. All eight missions were flown at medium altitude, no enemy aircraft were encountered or strafing

B-26 *The Mad Russian* with ground crew at Great Dunmow in August 1943. *(USAF)*

B-26 *Loretta Young* drops her deadly load. *(USAF)*

Men of the 555th Bomb Squadron taking a break at Great Dunmow.

attempted. Thereafter the Invaders were 'returned to depots' with a list of modifications that would delay full deployment by the 386th Group until 1945.

In October 1944 the 386th moved to Beaumont-sur-Oise (A-60), the last 9th Air Force bomber group to leave England for France. Great Dunmow was transferred to' the RAF and the station prepared to receive Nos 190 and 620 Stirling Squadrons in 38 Group. These units took part in Operation *Varsity* and after VE-Day the Stirlings were replaced by Halifaxes which served in a transport capacity. In December 1945 190 Squadron was disbanded at Great Dunmow and 620 Squadron left for the Mediterranean. In 1946 the Army used the airfield for storing hundreds of surplus military vehicles which were disposed of in auctions in 1947. For a few years, the grassed areas of the airfield were cut for grass meal and in 1960 farming operations commenced. In 1965/6 the concrete runways and other concrete was broken as hard core by St Ives Sand and Gravel for the new A12 highway.

A lasting reminder to the 322nd Bomb Group is B-26C 41-31773 *Flak Bait*, which flew in the 449th Bomb Squadron and racked up 202 missions. The fuselage is now preserved in the Smithsonian in Washington DC.

9

LITTLE WALDEN
(Hadstock)
(Station 165)

Little Walden Park and farms adjoining Hadstock Common formed the site for this bomber airfield which, originally, was named Hadstock. Construction began in the summer of 1942 with a target completion date of March the following year but most of the work was halted in the winter of 1942 and did not restart until May 1943 when the official name was changed to Little Walden. The main runway was 5,700 feet and the other two were standard at 4,200 feet long with fifty loop-type hardstandings. Two T2 hangars and domestic sites with accommodation for 2,894 personnel were built east of the airfield. The base was allocated for 8th Air Force use in August 1942 but passed to the 9th Air Force in October 1943.

The airfield officially opened on 6 March 1944. Next day the 409th Bomb Group – the second of the A-20 Havoc groups to join the 9th Air Force – arrived from the USA. This Group, which comprised the 640th, 641st, 642nd and 643rd Bomb Squadrons was commanded by Colonel Preston P. Pender, who remained in command until 4 July 1944, when Colonel Thomas R. Ford assumed command. Crews had been trained as a night-bomber unit, which immediately found itself with a shortage of night-qualified bombardier-navigators. This was remedied by transferring forty-nine officer bombardiers in from the B-26 Groups and re-training them. Meanwhile, ground crews had had to assemble aircraft that had come over from America as deck cargo. Once the work was completed the Group, originally trained in low-level attack, was soon busy flying formations and practising medium-altitude bombing from an optimum of 10,000 feet. Finally, on 13 April, when General Dwight D. Eisenhower was confirmed as Supreme Commander for the invasion and assumed control of all

Allied air operations from the United Kingdom, the 409th flew their first mission in the 97th Combat Wing.

After their first mission from Little Walden on 13 April over a hundred more were flown from the airfield. A total of ten A-20s were lost from Little Walden during this period. On 27 May 1944 the 409th Group led the attack on the marshalling yards at Amiens which controlled much of the traffic on the main lines serving Lille, Valenciennes and the Pas de Calais area as well as services south to Paris and Rouen. The yards lay within the eastern suburbs of Amiens, making accurate aiming essential, but 500 yards to the north, the River Somme, flowing east–west and parallel to the rail tracks, provided a reliable aiming point for the aircrews. Aiming-points were clearly defined for the bomber crews at briefings. All groups were involved in the maximum effort in which the Havoc force was to break the tracks, wreck switching gear and generally disable the yard, taking the locomotive depot as its aiming-point. The formation of thirty-eight 409th aircraft would form into two boxes, comprising thirty-four A-20Gs and four A-20J lead ships with bombardiers. A similar composition was despatched by the 410th, which comprised forty-three aircraft in two boxes, with thirty-eight G models and five A-20Js. Finally, there were forty-one aircraft from the 416th, consisting of three A-20Js and thirty-eight gun-nosed models, in two combat boxes. Fighter-bombers were to operate at the same time on diversionary sweeps, and the A-20s would have an escort of P-47s. Take-off time at group airfields was shortly after 1200 hours and the 409th A-20s would rendezvous with the 358th Fighter Group's Thunderbolts shortly afterwards.

The leading 640th Squadron formation made landfall at Le Treport and weak and inaccurate flak greeted the crews as they crossed into France. As they proceeded further into hostile territory, twenty-seven miles from the target at 11,500 feet near Formerie they encountered an intense and accurate flak barrage. Immediately the A-20G, the No. 3 plane in the leading element of three flown by 2nd Lieutenant Raymond L. Gregg in the 640th Bomb Squadron, was hit and spun out of the formation, narrowly missing the other Havocs before hitting the ground north-west of Forges-Les-Eaux. There were no survivors. This loss disrupted the formation and caused the flight to take wild evasive action in the face of flak that resulted in a further loss. Within two minutes the other two planes of the leading element were shattered by the flak. The A-20J-5 deputy lead ship piloted by Captain Leland F. Norton began a steep glide right after being hit and Norton was seen slumped over the

Little Walden flying control in 1944. The tower was purchased in 1982 by architect Roger Lynn and restored and converted to offices the following year. *(USAF)*

wheel. At about 5,000 feet one of the wings broke off and the plane spun into the ground, no parachutes being seen. FW 190s then intercepted the group, 1st Lieutenant Leon Robinson's gunner trading fire with one of the fighters before the German pilot gave up the chase.

On withdrawal, the A-20J-5 lead plane flown by Captain Leslie B. Huff had its left engine knocked out and Huff turned and headed for England while rapidly losing altitude. Five minutes from the French coast, knowing they were going down, he gave the signal to abandon the aircraft and the two gunners jumped. The bombardier-navigator was temporarily trapped in his compartment and by the time he freed himself the plane was over the Channel off Le Treport. The bombardier-navigator jumped and Huff prepared to follow. He removed his flak suit, crawled to the catwalk of the now blazing plane and his body struck the plane. He tried to pull the rip-cord with his right hand but found it impossible. He reached for the ripcord with his left hand, pulled it and the parachute opened. Two Spitfires maintained a close eye on proceedings as the Havoc settled and an ASR Sea Otter landed on the sea and picked up Huff and the bombardier-navigator from their dinghy and conveyed them to England. Meanwhile, with the loss of its leaders the first box broke up and the 409th decided to abandon the mission. Five Havocs made a 180-degree turn and flew back along their inbound track. Four other Havocs tacked onto another A-20 group's formation and came out with them. The other planes came out alone, one on a single engine just making it to an English airfield. Of the nineteen A-20s in the first box, three were lost and only two were undamaged. The second box also tacked on to the other A-20 group and followed them out; only two of its aircraft being damaged by flak.

That evening the 409th and the two other A-20 groups went to Amiens again. At 1900 hours thirty-three aircraft took off from Little Walden. As group lead Captain Roger D. Dunbar climbed out, nobody in his crew of four (which included the group photographer) saw another aircraft on a collision course. The leading A-20 had just risen over a wood beyond the east side of the airfield when it collided with a low-flying P-51. The Mustang disintegrated and the Havoc crashed in a meadow nearby. With its wheels still down, the A-20 had its entire tail unit severed by a P-51, which shed a wing as it went down to crash. The Havoc crashed with one survivor, Sergeant Angelo Mattei, who was pulled from the wreckage by a farmer's widow, thirty-seven-year-old Mrs Betty Everitt, who had seen the aircraft come down. She was trying to extricate another when part of the bomb-load exploded, killing both her and her little terrier which had come to the scene. Her bravery was commended by the US authorities and group personnel started a fund. The $3,000 that was raised was used later to help educate her young orphaned son Tony. The 409th carried on to the target, meeting intense barrage flak north-east of Formerie and then really heavy flak as they neared Amiens. Evasive action prevented any casualties, however, and the flights signalled 'bombs away' at 2035 hours.

The 409th Bomb Group began their journey to Brétigny (A-48) in France on 18 September and about ten days later, the 361st Fighter Group of the 8th Air Force moved in with its Mustangs. When part of this organisation was detached to the Continent, the 493rd Bomb Group's B-24 Liberators moved in while the runways at Debach were being repaired. After VE-Day, VIII Fighter Command retained Little Walden until late in 1945 for use by the 65th Fighter Wing Headquarters with final transfer back to the RAF being made on 30 January 1946. A large number of surplus US Army vehicles had been assembled on the airfield and resulted in government auctions over the next few years. In May 1958 the airfield was returned to agricultural use. The hangars remained and were used for storage and warehousing and the technical site was eventually used by light industries. Most of the runways were removed, but the bisected B1052 Saffron Walden to Linton road was re-opened, making use of part of the south-west/north-east runway. After remaining derelict for many years, the control tower was restored and is now a house.

10

MATCHING
(Station 166)

This bomber airfield was constructed by the 834th and 840th Engineer Battalions (Aviation), US Army, and it was originally planned to be ready to receive aircraft the following spring but it was only suitable for occupation in December 1943. There was a 6,000 feet main runway and two 4,200 feet runways with fifty loop hardstandings and two T2 hangars were eventually completed. To the south-east living accommodation – mostly Nissen huts – was built to house 2,282 personnel. At one time, the airfield was considered for enlargement with extended runways, for very heavy bomber use, but this plan never materialised.

On 3 January 1944 the 391st Bomb Group (M), commanded by Colonel Gerald 'Gerry' E. Williams of Presque Isle, Maine, left Hunter Field, Georgia, and the Marauder crews headed for Morrison Field in

Marauders in the 391st Bomb Group taxi out at Matching. *(USAF)*

The main runway at Matching airfield under construction near Mann Wood. *(USAF)*

The 834th and 840th Engineer Battalions (Aviation) built Matching airfield. Runways were laid in bays using dismountable metal shuttering. *(USAF)*

The 834th Engineering Battalion (Aviation) at work. *(USAF)*

Florida, then Borinquen in Puerto Rico, Atkinson in British Guyana and Belem and Natal in Brazil. Following a two-day stopover, the B-26s took off for Ascension Island. The next leg took them to Roberts Field in Liberia, where they arrived on 21 January. Each aircraft was given a thorough overhaul before the crews embarked on their next leg, which took them to Marrakesh, Morocco, where they arrived on the 22nd. The Marauders encountered bad weather and after one day's delay they departed for St Mawgan in Cornwall. On 30 January the first Marauders landed at Matching and the others arrived over the next few days, the last finally arriving on 24 February. The 391st Bomb Group became the fifth Marauder group to join IX Bomber Command, becoming a part of the 98th Wing.

After flying a few practice missions over the Midlands and the North Sea, on 15 February Field Order 202 alerted the Group to ready thirty-six Marauders for an attack on Beaumont-le-Roger aerodrome. The B-26s took off on schedule and set course to rendezvous with their RAF fighter escort before crossing into France but cloud began to build and made accurate bombing impossible so as flak opened up half-heartedly the Marauders turned for home. Having penetrated as far as France, the Group was at least allowed a mission credit. On 23 February two missions were scheduled and the 391st Bomb Group dispatched B-26s out in the morning and afternoon. The earlier mission resulted in the fighter escort being forced to head for home low on fuel, probably after trying to skirt around the overcast. Now alone the Marauders made 'a forty-minute tour of France' but luckily

Handing over of Station 166 at Matching on 4 March 1944. *(USAF)*

they escaped the attention of any enemy fighters. Both missions were aborted because of 10/10th cloud cover and most of the crews brought their bombs back and some jettisoned them over the sea.

The Group's next mission was on 24 February when thirty-six Marauders in the 391st Bomb Group attacked Gilze-Rijen airfield. The Group bombed in two box formations, the first releasing from 12,000 feet and the second from 11,500 feet. The 391st had scored direct hits on four or five aircraft shelters and several other buildings and made holes in the south–north runway. Slight battle damage was sustained by two aircraft, the flak being described as 'moderate and accurate'. A total of 151 missions were flown from Matching during which twenty B-26s were missing in action. On 28 May 1944 B-26s of the 391st and 344th Groups took off in the late afternoon to bomb the Amiens marshalling yards bombed the previous day by the Havocs. Following take-off and form-up the formation headed into France, with the twenty-eight B-26s of the 391st in the lead and thirty-seven 344th aircraft following. Their briefed route took the Marauders out across Beachy Head; over France they would make for Rouen and Amiens. Approaching the IP north-west of Hornoy the Marauders encountered flak and one burst under the right wing of the B-26B in the 573rd Squadron, flown by 1st Lieutenant Harry D. Porter. Oil began to spurt out of the right engine and Porter began to drop back before pulling up before the B-26 started to peel off right over Lieutenant Clark's B-26, which was forced to drop out of formation to avoid a collision. The damaged Marauder levelled-out apparently back under control, but it was losing altitude. It crossed back under the flight, going down. By then the 391st was at the IP and the formation began a turn that would take it into Amiens. Porter's Marauder eventually was lost to sight in cloud. All seven of Porter's crew were listed as MIA but six parachutes were apparently observed by watchers on the ground. Most of the Group achieved 'good' bombing ratings at Amiens but one of the flights in the second box placed every one of its bombs in open fields beyond the town.

On 20 June the 391st Bomb Group flew its 100th mission and John A. Moore the Group Chaplain flew the mission in a B-26 named *Rationed Passion* without noticing the name before the take-off. Mischievous friends had arranged to have a photograph taken upon his return in front of the Marauder, in order to send it, they insisted, to the *Florida Baptist Witness*, the Chaplain's home religious periodical. 'I told them to go ahead and send it' the Chaplain said and he meant it, his friends said. 'My reputation isn't that frail but I did wonder just

An 88-mm flak burst badly damaged the tail area of B-26C 42-107740 in the 391st Bomb Group on 20 May 1944. *(USAF)*

B-26 *Wogpatter* in the 391st Bomb Group at Matching. *(USAF)*

B-26 *Skeeter* in the 391st Bomb Group at Matching. *(USAF)*

B-26B 42-95836 *McCarty's Party* in the 572nd Bomb Squadron taxiing round the perimeter track at Matching on 8 March 1944. *(USAF)*

how the Chief Chaplain would have reacted if I, definitely a non-combatant, had been taken prisoner on a combat mission! As soon as it could be prepared, Chaplain Moore was awarded a medal inscribed: 'To Chaplain John Moore for Extraordinary Rationed Passion'. Major Harry A. Franck a sixty-two-year-old visiting PRO noted that:

Horseplay aside, the chaplain must have appreciated that the name of this ship was comparatively innocuous and one whose significance any chaplain could readily understand. It could have been *Valkyrie* for instance, which was depicted as a voluptuous nude of 'Pettyesque' proportions. *Valkyrie*, the crew learned was 'one of the maidens of Odin, awful and beautiful, who hover over the field of battle, choosing those to be slain and conducting the worthy to Valhalla'. Guns, bombsights, cameras and other items of flight equipment were frequently given names. Painted bombs on the fuselage indicated the number of missions. A duck meant a diversion flight in support of another formation; a doughnut [which the American Red Cross girls served from

B-26 *The Susan Kay* and Captain 'Skip' Roeper's crew in the 391st Bomb Group at Matching. (USAF)

B-26 *Rationed Passion* in the 391st Bomb Group at Matching. *(USAF)*

B-26 *Lady Chance* in the 391st Bomb Group at Matching. *(USAF)*

'Doughnut Wagons'] stood for a non-combat mission, either because of a SNAFU [Situation Normal All Fouled Up] or because it was only flown for practice.

In true tabloid style the various crewmen's names were painted in large letters, opposite such gangland pseudonyms as *Triggerman*, *Fingerman* and *Rodman*. A Major Wray, an expectant father, dubbed his ship *Wray & Son* only to be made a liar by a contrary stork. A ship whose entire crew had parents who had emigrated to America was named *Johnny Come Lately*. Then there was *Truman's Folly*, a slap at the unfavourable report of the Truman Committee early in 1943, on the B-26. The Truman report aroused a furore over the number of accidents in training cited in the second mission by B-26s in the ETO when none of the ten planes over the target got back, as proof that the B-26s were not fit to fly.

Franck remembered the 'nasty names fliers once called this B-26 airplane': the 'flying prostitute' because its short wings, in the early models, had 'no visible means of support'; the 'widow maker' the 'flying-coffin', 'the electric chair with a throttle'. This was the plane that gave rise to the saying, 'A plane a day in Tampa Bay' which was only too nearly, literally true for its early pilots were trained at MacDill Field, Florida. But Marauder pilots came to like the B-26 and were proud to fly a 'hot' airplane.'

Major Franck later, in France, flew a mission with the Group he called the 'Black Death', which lost sixteen B-26s to FW 190s on a mission to a railway aqueduct at Ahrweiler, Germany, on 23 December 1944. The 391st Bomb Group had completed its move to Roye-Amy (A-73) in late September 1944 and this was the end of Matching airfield's association with the 9th Air Force as a combat airfield. C-47s of IX Troop Carrier Command were detached to Matching later in 1944 for exercises with British paratroops. Next came the Stirlings of the training unit for the airborne force, which remained until 1946.

Returned to agricultural use, the concrete was soon removed for road hardcore but the hangar on the technical site survived for farm use. However, in the late eighties it was dismantled and re-erected at North Weald for 'Aces High' where it was used for TV productions. The control tower still stands and for some years was used for radar experiments by Cossor Electronics. Part of a runway is now used as a public road and another surviving portion was used for heavy goods vehicle instruction. Rowe Brothers of Rookwood Hall, whose family owned most of the land on which the airfield was built, remain the major farmers.

B-26 *Pink Lady II* **in the 391st Bomb Group at Matching.** *(USAF)*

11

RAYDON
(Station 157)

Although designed as a standard bomber base the only airfield in Suffolk allocated for 9th Air Force use was used purely by fighter groups. Raydon was built by the 833rd and 862nd Engineer Battalions (Aviation) of the US Army in 1942–3. Runways were one of 6,000 feet and two of 4,200 feet and there were fifty loop-type hardstandings and one pan, two T2 hangars and seven dispersed domestic sites for 2,842 personnel to the south-east and nearly all in the village of Great Wenham. The bomb-dump was situated in Raydon Great Wood to the north of the flying field. Farms and houses were requisitioned and demolished, changing the look of the village for ever. Raydon was to be one of the last airfields of its type to be constructed in England during the war. Locals remember the village street being constantly full of trucks on the move. The road was not hard surfaced and quickly became a sea of mud. Construction started with considerable optimism

Men of the 833rd Engineer Battalion (Aviation) laying French drains.
(USAF)

Men of the 833rd Engineer Battalion (Aviation) unloading rolls of steel mesh. *(USAF)*

Men of the 833rd Engineer Battalion (Aviation) laying PSP. Raydon was built by the 833rd and 862nd Engineer Battalions (Aviation) and the 833rd also constructed eight domestic sites at Gosfield to the south-west of the airfield. *(USAF)*

and little thought of the problems lying ahead, so the completion date for the entire project was set at 1 January 1943. It was common knowledge among the less careful observers that the entire Battalion would 'certainly be home by Christmas'.

By the latter part of September 1942, Nissen hut living sites had been partially completed for each company and labelled with such names as 'Greenwich Village', 'Youngstown', 'Dodge City' and 'Powder River'. The entire airfield was christened 'Camp Chicago' but received the official title of USAAF Station 157. When personnel had been moved inside out of the rain, attention was turned to the job at hand; and during the ensuing fourteen months the Battalion laboured twenty-four hours a day (three eight-hour shifts) through heat, cold, rain and shine on the construction of Raydon airfield. Construction equipment arrived, but only in a trickle, from the USA, so British substitutes were employed – supply and maintenance long remained critical problems. Inexperience was overcome only as time passed. As winter set in the entire project became bogged down in a quagmire of 'good ol' Limey mud' and it was only through strict mud control that operations were able to continue. In an effort to circumvent this problem, Company A constructed and operated for three months their 'secret weapon', their 'Beeler, Benson, and Blue' railroad, a half mile of narrow gauge track with a diesel engine and cars for hauling

Laying steel mesh. *(USAF)*

concrete. As problems arose on all sides, the completion date faded further and further into the distance and, with a more practical outlook, it was announced in December 1942, that an attempt would be made to complete the first runway, known as the 'Pulaski Skyway,' by 1 February 1943.

As the year drew to a close the Battalion spent its first Christmas in England. On the afternoon of 24 December, Company B had about eighty children from the adjacent homes to a party at which they were entertained by 'GI' talent and treated to candy, peanuts, and doughnuts under the direction of Sergeant Cantrell and 'Lord' Luton. Some of the men were invited to English homes for the holidays. Mr Guy, the American Red Cross representative, secured a Christmas goodie bag for all members of the Battalion. It was not a 'merry' Christmas and it was not like the ones the men were accustomed to enjoying at home, but they were not in England to eat plum pudding and sing carols – they had a mission to accomplish and, as the Battalion Commander said, '...the war is just one year nearer to being ended than it was last Xmas'.

In spite of rain, snow, cold, and a sea of mud, with dogged determination the Battalion surmounted countless obstacles and drove relentlessly forward toward its first goal, the completion of 'Pulaski

A Mobile Concrete Mixer used by the 834th Engineer Battalion (Aviation) at Matching on 13 June 1943. *(USAF)*

Men of the 833rd Engineer Battalion (Aviation) laying runway surfaces. *(USAF)*

P-47 Thunderbolt *Betty* in the 358th Fighter Group at Raydon in January 1944. *(USAF)*

Skyway' by 1 February 1943. As the unit began to get the feel of the work, operations proceeded more smoothly and more rapidly. On 17 January 1943, to quote *The Mud City Gazette*, the men of Company B '...took the bit in their teeth, and went "all out" to pour 961 linear feet of 20-foot wide concrete slab in one day. Three weeks later they put down one 1,075 feet'. With favourable weather and the advantage of experience which the Battalion had gained during the past months, on 1 May Company A smashed all previous records by pouring out a 1,228 feet in one day! Meanwhile, other records were also being broken. On 17 February a crew from Headquarters and Service Company ran off 116 batches of concrete at the Boot Hill mixer to almost double the previous record. On 13 March they turned out 161 batches and on 7 May, all previous records for batches turned out anywhere on the job were shattered when Company A ground out 453 batches at Devil's Kitchen.

Such work produced results. The first goal was reached; and Major Beeler was writing in *The Mud City Gazette*:

We did it! It wasn't easy, but there lies one full runway, 720 feet longer than one mile and any day a B-17 or a B-24 wants to land, all we have to do is clear the runway, and wave him in. What is more important – we did it on schedule – with exactly thirty minutes to spare. By 1 October 1943 the entire site was classed as being 71 per cent complete whereas the schedule called for it to be 87% finished. A total of 1,175,000 man hours of labour had been expended and 875,000 man hours of work accomplished.

Late in November 1943 the partly completed airfield received the 357th Fighter Group commanded by Colonel Henry R. Spicer, which had trained on P-39 Airacobras in the US but was selected as the second group to be equipped with the P-51B Mustang. Only six Mustangs were available for pilot training by Christmas and early in January 1944 more were received but, although some pilots flew with the 354th Fighter Group at Boxted to gain experience – one failing to return on 25 January – they did not become operational. The 8th Air Force desperately needed Mustangs for long-range fighter support for its bombers and on the last day of January the 358th Fighter Group commanded by Colonel Cecil L. Wells and its P-47 Thunderbolts were exchanged for the 357th and its Mustangs. The 358th had arrived in England on 29 November and had become operational on 20 December. The 357th Fighter Group moved to Leiston. The 358th flew its first mission from Raydon on 3 February. The P-47s were already flying escort missions and they continued to do so even though transferred to the Tactical Air Force. During thirty-two missions flown while at Raydon the Group was credited with eight enemy aircraft destroyed for the loss of four P-47s.

As spring approached, fighter-bombing operations became more

Swinging the prop on P-47 Thunderbolt *Chunky* in the 358th Fighter Group. *(USAF)*

frequent and on 13 April 1944 the 358th moved to High Halden, one of the advanced landing grounds in Kent. Raydon was transferred to the 8th Air Force with the arrival from Metfield of the 353rd Fighter Group. This Group was at the time one of the most successful P-47 groups in Eighth Fighter Command and was commanded by Colonel Glenn Duncan, already a distinguished ace. This Group remained at Raydon until the end of the war. (See *Fighter Bases of WWII: 8th Air Force USAAF 1943–45.*) On 20 December 1945 Raydon was transferred to RAF Fighter Command, although no further flying units were stationed at the airfield. A small part of the airfield was sold in 1952 and the station closed officially on 8 August 1958.

12

RIVENHALL
(Station 168)

This airfield, two miles north of the village after which it was named, was largely in the vicinity of Silver End and Little Coggeshall. Construction was begun in early 1943 with the runways, perimeter and fifty-one loop hardstandings being built by Messrs W. & C. French and the two T2 hangars and dispersed accommodation for 2,594 personnel to the south-east by Bovis Limited. A 6,000 feet main runway and two of 4,200 feet were standard. Building progress was slow during the autumn and winter of 1943, so much so that much of the accommodation and support installations were not finished when the first units of the USAAF arrived. The airfield had first been allocated to the 8th Air Force for heavy bomber use and eventually re-assigned to the 3rd Bomb Wing, which became the nucleus of IX Bomber Command.

On 22 January 1944 the 382nd Fighter Squadron in the 363rd

Shark-tooth B-26 Marauder 44-67918 in the 397th Bomb Group in 1944. *(Robert Astrella)*

B-26B-55-MA 42-96138 U2-C *By-Golly*, the leading B-26 in the 598th Bomb Squadron, 397th Bomb Group, formation received a 'hot' reception over a French bridge on 16 July 1944 when an engine was disabled, the hydraulic reservoir hit and the rudder control severed by flak. Captain Quinn West (right with propeller) managed to bring the Marauder down for a crash-landing at A-7 (Azeville), a Normandy airstrip where all nine men, including two special radio operators, escaped a fire. Captain West, who received the DFC for this action, was deeply religious and never swore, hence 'By Golly'. *(USAF)*

Fighter Group arrived from Keevil where it had been awaiting equipment for the past month. The Group had been selected as the third in the ETO to be equipped with the new P-51B Mustang. The squadron received Mustangs to begin training two days later. The remaining 380th and 381st Fighter Squadrons arrived by the end of the

By-Golly – burnt out after the crash-landing at A-7 (Azeville). *(USAF)*

The crew of *By-Golly*. **Captain Quinn West (standing second from left) was killed on 1 August when his aircraft was shot down by fighters.** *(USAF)*

first week of February. Many of the Mustangs had already seen service with the 354th Fighter Group at Boxted, having been withdrawn for modification and re-issued. The early model Mustangs had been employed in a tactical fighter reconnaissance role by the RAF and USAAF and the same task was planned for the new P-51B. However, its exceptional endurance and good performance made the type ideal for long-range bomber escort duties, which was the pressing need of the USAAF in Britain at this time.

Bad weather caused the 363rd Fighter Group's first combat mission to be abandoned, but this was flown two days later, on 24 February, when twenty-four P-51s took off from Rivenhall for Belgium on bomber support. An attempt by the heavies to bomb Berlin on 3 March was thwarted by bad weather and was aborted but the 363rd Fighter Group claimed 2-1-2 enemy aircraft. Next day, in the Berlin area, the

Yellow-nosed B-26B 42-96165, which was known as the *Big Hairy Bird* in the 599th Bomb Squadron, 397th Bomb Group, with shark teeth. When the aircraft was later transferred to the 558th Bomb Squadron, 387th Bomb Group, shortly before the end of the war a 'tiger tail' stripe was added. *(USAF)*

group either became lost in the clouds that covered the area or were jumped over Germany by the *Luftwaffe* and eleven Mustangs failed to return to Rivenhall. The 363rd continued to provide escort for 8th Air Force heavies, but fighter-bomber missions also were flown. This included dive-bombing and several practice sorties were despatched to dive-bomb targets in the Stour estuary. On two occasions, the Mustangs involved broke up attempting to pull out of the dive which led to re-examination of the technique employed. During its stay at

HQ building at Rivenhall. *(USAF)*

A formation of 397th Bomb Group B-26 Marauders painted in invasion stripes. *(USAF)*

Rivenhall the 363rd Fighter Group flew twenty missions, lost sixteen aircraft in action and was credited with the destruction of thirteen enemy aircraft.

On 14 April 1944, as part of a general movement of 9th Air Force fighter units in the Colchester area to the advanced landing grounds, the 363rd Fighter Group moved to Staplehurst and the first of sixty B-26s of the 397th Bomb Group arrived from Gosfield. The 397th flew its first combat mission on 20 April when nearly 400 B-26s and A-20s attacked gun emplacements, V-1 launch sites, Poix airfield and targets of opportunity. Led by Colonel Coiner, the thirty-six B-26s of the 397th Group bombed a V-1 site at Le Plouy Ferme in the Pas de Calais. Following on from their attempts against *Noball* targets the 397th Bomb Group Marauders flew their eighth and ninth missions on April 28 and 29 when they set out to bomb a large marshalling yard just outside Paris at Mantes Gassicourt, but on both occasions cloud covered the target. In order to avoid casualties to the French population there were strict instructions not to bomb unless the target was clearly visible and so the Group brought their bombs home.

On 8 May the 397th first got to grips with one of bridge targets in France. Although in the early part of the bridge campaign there was often only light anti-aircraft fire to contend with at the bridges, the Germans had moved radar-predicted heavy flak guns to protect them and losses for the Allied bombers began to mount steadily. On their

A box of Marauders in the 597th Bomb Squadron, 397th Bomb Group, over England. *(USAF)*

fourteenth mission thirty-eight Marauders of the 397th encountered heavy flak when they approached a railway bridge across the Seine at Oissel near Rouen, which accounted for the first Group aircraft to be shot down in combat. All the crew parachuted to safety and became PoWs. Only twenty-four aircraft bombed the target and a total of twenty-six aircraft were found to be flak damaged on return to Rivenhall. More successful missions against a further eight Seine bridges followed at the end of the month during five days of concentrated action from 27–31 May, fortunately without loss. From then on the 397th gained an impressive reputation for their precision attacks against bridges, earning themselves the unofficial title of *The Bridge Busters*.

On 28 May on the mission to bomb the Maissons Lafitte rail bridge across the Seine on the outskirts of Paris, twenty-one of the Group's Marauders returned with flak damage but the south span of the bridge was dropped into the river.

Captain Sam Steere, pilot of *Hi Ho Silver*, who flew fifty-five missions in the 598th Bombardment Squadron during his tour of duty, described the methods adopted when attacking bridges – or any of the other heavily defended targets.

The whole evasive tactic for the B-26 was based upon tight formation flying. We flew in one direction for about 30 seconds (when under fire) which was long enough for the German fire control equipment to track us, determine the shell time of flight and cut the fuse time, then we would make a random movement left or right and hope to have the entire box of 18 ships displaced sufficiently during the 15 or 20 seconds of time remaining before the shells exploded in our vicinity. Naturally on the bomb run we had to fly straight and level and there 'we took our lumps'. A good leader could continue the random evasive movements in such a manner as to roll out on the bomb run with a minimum but sufficient time to effectively drop the bombs. A good leader was life insurance and there was no place for eager well-meaning but inexperienced flight leaders. With sufficient ground defence so that a box barrage could be put up it was 'Katie bar the door' – we just hoped to be lucky and get through with minimum losses while getting to the target so that we didn't have to go back again. With a full bomb load the ships couldn't fly much higher than about 12,000 feet, which didn't leave much room for any bad luck!

Between 12 to 24 May the 397th attacked seven German coastal defence targets and continued to do so in the first three days in June, culminating on D-Day 6 June with a 'maximum effort' mission in support of the landings in Normandy. Crews were roused at 0200 hours and briefing quickly followed. The Marauders had to be over the targets at precisely 0609 hours – twenty-one minutes before the first landing craft grounded on the beaches. A record number of fifty-three Group aircraft took off from Rivenhall in the early hours and joined other Marauder and Havoc squadrons, to provide a total of 276 bombers. They had all been briefed to attack seven defensive positions off *Utah* Beach a few minutes before the US 4th Infantry Division stormed ashore at 0630 hours. The 397th Bomb Group B-26s dropped to 3,500 feet to try to see the objective and when the position came into view the Group bombed at the set time before the first troops waded ashore. Following a hectic few minutes in one of the most crowded pieces of sky on that memorable morning, their mission accomplished, the Groups turned for home. Landing back in England some of the crews of the 397th prepared to fly their second mission of the day, this time against coastal defences at Trouville, on the other end of the invasion beaches.

B-26B 42-96142 *Dee-Feater* **in the 596th Bomb Squadron, 397th Bomb Group, at Rivenhall flown by Lieutenant Colonel Robert L. McLeod, the squadron CO, over England in July 1944. The aircraft was named in honour of McLeod's wife Dee and it acted as the lead ship on many missions in the summer of 1944. McLeod flew twenty-seven missions as box leader from Rivenhall, many of them in** *Dee-Feater***. (***Charles E. Brown***)**

On 24 June the 397th Bomb Group flew its fifty-eighth mission when it returned to France to bomb the Maissons Lafitte rail bridge once more. A terrific flak barrage greeted the Marauders of the 397th as they commenced their bomb run, as Sergeant Neil McGinnis, engineer-gunner in Captain Steere's crew recalls.

June 24 was my 24th mission and we really caught it this time. We were flying in the second box and flak started coming up about 15 miles before we reached the target. Four aircraft from the first box went down right off and I saw every ship around us had an engine throwing smoke and by the time we got to the target ours was the only one that wasn't smoking. We salvoed our bombs and swung off to the right over Paris although we

Crew of B-26B-55-MA 42-96191 9F-N *The Milk Run Special* in the 597th Bomb Squadron, 397th Bomb Group, pose for the camera with a 1,000-lb bomb. This Marauder, which has forty-three mission symbols on the fuselage, finished the war and completed more than 100 combat missions. *(USAF)*

B-26 42-96078 *Slightly Dangerous* **in the 599th Bomb Squadron, 397th Bomb Group, which was destroyed on 17 June 1944.** *(USAF)*

were supposed to go left but there was too much flak in that direction, Out of nowhere other B-26s fell in alongside to join us. When we got back to Rivenhall our right governor was out and the prop was in fixed pitch. I took off for the bomb bay and just managed to hand-crank the flaps down as we made our landing. As we slid off the runway others were coming in right and left – one jumped a ditch and they had to build a bridge to get it back across. Every ship was hit except one. What a life!

Apart from the four already mentioned, two other B-26s had crashed in friendly territory and twenty-five crew members were reported missing. Out of the six aircraft a total of seven crew members died, the remainder were either PoW or safe. For the 397th Bomb Group Marauders it had been an exceptional day, although the Group had been fortunate in one respect as the German gunners missed both of the lead aircraft. Following the mission there was a five-day lull for the Group because of poor weather.

On 1 August the 397th Bomb Group dispatched thirty-six aircraft on their eighty-third mission against a bridge near Angers over the River Loire. Because the bridges were always heavily defended by the German flak batteries it was not unusual to say the least when the three boxes led by McLeod, West and Taylor found themselves under fire from a number of Bf 109s and FW 190s as they began their approach to the bridge. Disregarding the escort of P-51 Mustangs, the determined German fighters pressed home their attack and the Marauder flown by Captain West was singled out for special attention, receiving several hits. A blaze started in the cockpit and smoke and confusion on the flight deck increased. West wrestled to hold the stricken ship steady as he gave the bale-out signal. Of the nine-man crew seven parachuted to safety and became PoWs but West and his navigator were killed, the B-26 crashing in a French meadow. It was only the third time that the 397th had been in combat with the *Luftwaffe* since they began flying missions in April. During the 111 days the 397th were at Rivenhall the 397th flew eighty-six combat missions, thirty-two of these attacks on bridges. Other targets were enemy airfields, rail junctions, fuel and ammunition stores, V-weapon sites and various military installations in France and the Low Countries. During these missions, a total of sixteen B-26s were missing in action and several others wrecked in crash-landings at the base.

In order to increase its radius of combat action the 397th went on 24 July to Hurn in Hampshire as the break-out of the Allied forces from the Normandy beachhead meant that potential targets were diminishing. At Hurn the Group added a further twenty-one missions

Marauders in the 397th Bomb Group on the line at Rivenhall on 24 November 1943. *(USAF)*

to their tally, followed by a move to A-26 at Gorges in France on the last day of August. During September they were joined by the other Marauder groups of the 9th, occupying former *Luftwaffe* bases on the Continent as the Allied armies pushed forward. Rivenhall airfield meanwhile was made available to the Allied airborne forces. In early October Stirlings of 295 Squadron RAF arrived with most of its operations consisting of supply drops to Norwegian resistance forces and similar activities over Holland and Denmark. On 24 March 1945 the unit took part in Operation *Varsity*, the crossing of the Rhine. Early in April another Stirling squadron arrived, 570 Squadron, which joined 295 Squadron in night operations in support of resistance forces in occupied countries. In the autumn of 1944 Rivenhall was one of the four vacated Essex airfields taken over by 38 Group, RAF. Replacing the Marauders came two squadrons of Stirling four-engined bombers, recent survivors of the Arnhem operation, now performing the task of Horsa glider towing tugs and dropping supplies to the resistance groups in Occupied Europe. Both 295 and 570 Squadrons were to remain at Rivenhall until January 1946 when the airfield finally closed, whereupon the station was held on a care and maintenance basis. Buildings on the Rivenhall site were used by the local authorities at the end of the war as a home for displaced Polish personnel and later as a hostel for travellers of the road.

In June 1956 Marconi leased the two main hangars and some other huts for their work in connection with radar development and within ten years had taken over most of the surviving buildings. This ensured that several of the wartime buildings including the station cinema and power house were largely unchanged and are still standing today. Although much of the main runway has been retained the two smaller runways and the greater part of the concrete perimeter track were removed and used as hard core in the road building programme of the 1960s when the A12 London road to the east coast was upgraded.

13

SNAILWELL, CAMBS
(Station 361)

The station, which occupies 150 acres of free-draining grassland just north-east of Newmarket on the Cambridgeshire/Suffolk border, opened as a satellite for Duxford in the spring of 1941 and it was used by a variety of RAF fighter and Army co-operation squadrons until October 1942 when the P-39 Airacobras of the US 347th Fighter Squadron arrived from Duxford. They left in early December, but not before two of the Airacobras had crashed on the airfield. During the busy period prior to the launch of the cross-Channel invasion, IX Air Force Service Command's facilities at 3rd Tactical Air Depot Grove became overloaded and Snailwell airfield was acquired from the Air Ministry for temporary occupation by Mobile Repair and Reclamation Squadrons (MR & R).

On 7 May 1944 the 41st Base Complement Squadron moved in to undertake the necessary housekeeping duties, although an RAF section remained. The next day the 33rd and 41st Mobile Repair and Reclamation Squadrons arrived, most personnel being accommodated under canvas. From mid-May Douglas A-20 Havocs were flown in and there were often a dozen on the airfield at any one time. The mechanics' task was to carry out certain theatre modifications and ready the Havocs for operational use as a reserve. The 41st MR & R Squadron was not required for this work and after two weeks moved out to Grove. Their place was taken by the 51st Service Squadron which specialised in A-20 maintenance. Early in July the situation at Grove was sufficiently improved for the A-20 operation to be transferred. The 51st Service Squadron left on 12 July and the 33rd MR & R Squadron followed, leaving on the 26th. The two remaining Havocs were collected before the end of the month. The RAF vacated Snailwell in 1946, since when the A45 Newmarket bypass has cut through the former airfield. For many years a solitary Blister hangar, used as a farm shelter, remained close to this road. Much of the land not in arable production has been turned into paddocks for the racehorse studs nearby.

STANSTED MOUNTFITCHET
(Station 169)

First allocated to the 8th Air Force in August 1942, the following October it was selected to serve as an advanced air depot and so construction of twenty-four aircraft hardstandings and more T2 hangars and workshops on the east side of the airfield at Takeley were begun by the 817th Engineer Battalion. They would have been unaware that fifty years later their early efforts would culminate in the establishment of London's third airport at Stansted with one of the world's most modern terminal buildings. When they were sent to North Africa in the spring of 1943, the 825th Engineer Battalion took over, joined by the 850th, and these units completed the airfield by the end of the year. The 825th Engineer Battalion completed the

Lieutenant B. W. Seth flew the 344th Bomb Group B-26 Marauder *Mary Ann* at Stansted in 1944. When the Group transferred to the Continent after D-Day, *Mary Ann* went with it and survived the war with over 100 missions. (*Jack Havener*)

Dellwin Bentley, the 497th Bomb Squadron CO in the 344th Bomb Group who always wore cowboy boots, on top of *Hard To Get*. (USAF)

construction of airfield roads, as well as the control tower, Fire Station and Motor Transport Section before leaving in December 1943. Final work on the military airfield's runways and taxiways began in May 1943 with the arrival of the 850th Engineer Battalion who remained at Stansted until April 1944. A 6,000 feet main runway and the two 4,200 feet runways were put down and there were forty-eight loop hardstandings and two pans with domestic accommodation for 2,658 personnel. The airfield and associated areas covered about 3,000 acres and was the largest 9th Air Force base in East Anglia.

Officially opened on 7 August 1943 when the 30th Air Depot Group arrived, the base was transferred to the 9th Air Force on 16 October. Although the official name was Stansted Mountfitchet, after the large village lying a mile to the north-west, the base was normally referred to as Stansted. On 8 February 1944 the first B-26 Marauders of the 344th Bomb Group arrived with its 494th, 495th, 496th and 497th

Men of the 850th Engineering Battalion undergoing battle training at Stansted. *(US Army)*

Squadrons, to prepare for its combat debut under group commander Colonel Reginald F. C. Vance of San Antonio, Texas. The sea journey from the United States took around twelve days and nights. The vessels used were often Liberty Ships able to carry about two thousand men. Ports of arrival were usually Gourock in Scotland, or Liverpool. The Americans were always pleased to be back on dry land after crossing the Atlantic Ocean but they then had to endure long train journeys to Bishop's Stortford Station, before boarding trucks for the

Sad Sack **taking off on a night mission.** *(USAF)*

B-26 Marauder *Sad Sack* and personnel at Stansted. *(USAF)*

final short journey to Stansted. The GIs' personal recollections recall the strange experience of travelling at night, through towns darkened by the war-time black-out. They soon realised that the war was very close to English people with nearly every other man in uniform and many women working in jobs previously done by the men. The visible evidence of German bombing also gave the Americans their first experience of the reality of war.

Seventy Marauders were on hand by the beginning of March. On the 6th the Group flew its first mission, sending thirty-seven Marauders to bomb Bernay-St-Martin aerodrome. There were no crew casualties and four Marauders received slight flak damage. The next day the Group bombed the airfield at Conches and the results were described as 'very good'. On the 8th the 344th sent fifty-four Marauders on the raid on Volkel and Soesterberg airfields in Holland. During the take-off and climb to get above a low cloud ceiling the aircraft flown by 1st Lieutenant John K. Eckert and Captain Jack W. Miller collided in the murk. All twelve crew members died. The bombing at Soesterberg was described as 'good', the 344th dropping 571 100-lb and forty-nine 500-lb bombs in the face of intense flak, which hit fourteen aircraft. Later PR coverage confirmed that they had 'hit the place hard'.

Bonnie Langford singing at a US Special Services Show at Stansted in 1944. *(USAF)*

People in the Stansted area soon developed friendships with the GIs after their arrival and the American servicemen quickly grew fond of the many hospitable pubs in and around Stansted and Bishop's Stortford and 'The Ash' at Burton End and Stansted's 'Dog & Duck' still look today very similar to their traditional appearance then, despite some modernisation. The 'Barley Mow' in Stansted is now a private house, while in Bishop's Stortford, only the 'Nag's Head' survives, the 'Reindeer' and 'Grapes' pubs having long since made way for more shops. Saturday night dances in Long's Ballroom, Bishop's Stortford, were very popular despite the occasional 'friendly punch-ups'. Long's remained an important centre for social activities for many years after the war, until it too was demolished in 1988 to make room for a modern shopping arcade. Another popular venue was the 'Causeway' in Bishop's Stortford which opened in 1943 as a special hostel and canteen for American servicemen. The club had accommodation for 300 'residents' together with large lounges, a reading room, dining room and barber's shop, tailor's shop and shower rooms. A local newspaper of that period reported that The Lord Lieutenant of Essex received from the Commanding Officers of various American Units stationed in the county the most remarkable tributes to the kindness of the people of Essex at Christmas time 1943.

A typical extract, quoted from a letter by a Brigadier General stated, 'The County of Essex has been most kind to us throughout our stay. We have all made many good friends here, whom we will remember with pleasure in many years to come.' The hospitality of the people of Essex was reciprocated by the Americans in many ways, including participation in a special War Orphans Fund, organised by the *Stars & Stripes* newspaper and as a result, the 344th Engineering Battalion adopted a local nine-year-old orphan, whose parents had been killed in an air raid.

The 344th Bomb Group participated in over 100 missions from Stansted, losing twenty-six Marauders in action. The first mission was flown on 29 February and the last from Stansted on 30 September when the Group moved to Cormeilles-en-Vexin (A-59), France. On 28 May the target for thirty-six of the Group's Marauders was the Mantes-Gassincourt railway bridge but only nineteen B-26s were able to bomb accurately and five of the aircraft were shot down. On D-Day on 6 June at first light the 344th Bomb Group led four groups in the assault by the IX Bomber Command formations upon three coastal batteries at Beau Guillot, La Madeleine and St-Martin de Varreville at *Utah* Beach. The Marauders had to be over the targets at precisely 0609 hours – twenty-one minutes before the first landing craft grounded on the beaches. Most groups mounted a maximum effort of three boxes of eighteen aircraft each instead of the normal mission

B-26s at Stansted while hangar construction continues. (USAF)

Airfield construction equipment passing through Stansted Mountfitchet village. *(USAF)*

strength of two boxes with one gun emplacement the target of each box of bombers. At Stansted the first aircraft of the fifty-six that were dispatched took off at 0412 hours. In the lead was Major Jens A. Norgaard flying *Mary Jo*, named in honour of his wife. John K. Havener was flying as co-pilot in the deputy lead position of the third box.

> The orders were to bomb assigned targets in the clear regardless of how low the cloud cover forced us to descend. Since our normally efficient bombing altitude was 12,000 feet the prospect of going in at a much lower level was terrifying as we would be sitting ducks for light flak, machine gun and even rifle fire! Nevertheless, it was impressed upon us that the entire invasion plan hinged upon our hitting the targets assigned. If we failed, Operation *Overlord* failed! With the odds of altitude and flak against us and with no idea of what opposition the *Luftwaffe* would mount, we figured half of us would not make it back if forced to bomb at a low-level!
>
> Our groups actually bombed at from 7,250 down to 3,500 feet and finished doing so just three minutes prior to our troops

hitting the beaches at 0630 hours. The clouds were in layers varying from 8 to 9/10 coverage and topping out at 13,500 feet. With cloud bases down to 2,500 feet bombing in the clear was difficult at best from any altitude. All targets along *Utah* Beach were hit with results ranging from poor to excellent.

My group formed up in the rain and darkness, as did all the others. As we headed south the clouds broke somewhat and we managed to climb to about 8,000 feet but by the time we left the coast of England they began to thicken and all three boxes had to go down to 6,500, 5,500 and 3,700 feet respectively to bomb. Our target was gun positions on the high ground above *Utah* Beach at Beau Guillot and each ship carried 16 250lb general purpose bombs. The intent was not to knock out the gun positions but to stun the German gun crews and any infantry in the area, keeping them holed up, and to create a network of 'ready-made' foxholes which our troops could use once they'd gained a foothold on the beach. Three other bomb groups carried the same bomb load and bombed specific *Utah* Beach locations including the beach itself to explode mines, tear up barbed wire barricades and tank traps along with creating foxholes on the

B-26 Marauder makes a low pass over Stanstead. *(USAF)*

beach. The other four B-26 groups carried 1,000 and 2,000lb GP bombs and hit the coastal batteries at Ouistreham, Benerville, Pointe du Hoc and Maisy while the three Havoc groups, carrying 500lb demolition, GP and fragmentation bombs, hit a railroad junction near Valognes, German troop concentrations at Argentan and a marshalling yard at Carentan. Their targets were all inland in the areas where our paratroops had landed the night before.

On the beach the bombing window was so narrow that if we couldn't line up with the target on our first pass, we were to abort the drop and carry the bombs back home. There just wasn't enough time for anyone to make a second pass! Everyone dropped, as all were determined to make the mission a success! Our first troops hit the beach on schedule at exactly 0630 hours and the main phase of the invasion was on!

As our group approached the IP (Initial Point for starting the bomb run) we came to straight and level and then the German flak started coming up at us. One ship in our first box took a direct hit and did a complete snap roll but recovered and slid back into formation to continue the bomb run! Absolutely amazing since the B-26 was not an aerobatic aircraft! A ship in the low flight of our box also got hit and went down in flames. [On the target approach, flak claimed the B-26B flown by 2nd Lieutenant James B. McKamey, which was hit in the right engine and with a fire in its full bomb bay, the aircraft was pulled out of formation and turned to head back across the Channel, but the B-26 exploded in mid-air. Three parachutes were reported before the Marauder exploded.]

We dropped our bombs at 0609 hours and headed west across the peninsula to turn north near the Isle of Guernsey. As we flew northward the entire invasion panorama unfolded before us and we could see the ground fire of tracers and incendiaries squirting up into the groups following us, and the first waves of landing craft approaching the beaches. The largest military operation in the history of the world was awesome to behold!

We returned to our base in time for a second breakfast at 0830 hours and I can say for sure that this repast was relished much more than the earlier one at 0330! That one had taken on the form of a last meal before execution!

Amazingly, only three B-26s were shot down by flak out of

B26 landing at Stanstead. *(USAF)*

332 that actually bombed from the 424 that originally took off on the mission. Twenty aborted due to mechanical problems, only two were lost in a mid-air collision southeast of London and 67 couldn't bomb because of cloud cover obscuring their targets. Of 135 Havocs launched 132 bombed with three aborting due to mechanical trouble and only one was lost to flak. In spite of these figures, the entire mission was a success as we had done what was expected of us and it was all made possible by two things: 1. The cleverness of Allied Intelligence in convincing most of the German General Staff that the invasion would take place further up the coast in the Calais area where the Channel was only 20 miles wide. We caught them with their pants down! 2. The pre-invasion mission of the 9th to destroy *Luftwaffe* airfields and aircraft had paid off. Only 20 FW 190 fighters gave the 391st Group any opposition that morning and they shot down one of those! We lost no B-26s or A-20s to fighters!

Our group flew a second mission that afternoon, as did all the rest and some a third one, but I was not on the loading list so wasn't much concerned. This time they carried four 1,000lb GP bombs each and bombed gun positions in the Cherbourg area.

Marauders leaving their smoking target. *(USAF)*

What did concern me, as well as all Maraudermen who saw it, occurred about two weeks later when the first *Life* magazine printed after D-Day arrived from my wife. To preface this you should know that some of the same USAAF brass that put the 9th on the back-burner had unsuccessfully tried to brush the Martin B-26 Marauder off the stove top completely so as to use the North American B-25 Mitchell as the sole medium bomber of WWII. *Life* added insult to injury for Maraudermen as there was a full two-page spread in it with an artist's impression of the D-Day landings. It was a beautiful piece of black and white work and showed scores of landing craft heading toward Normandy from balloon-barraged harbours of southern England in the foreground and in the far-off background our Navy shelling shore fortifications above the landing zones while overhead formations of medium bombers were almost at their IPs and higher up the heavies were beginning to appear. It was all pretty much correct except that the medium bombers were all B-25s! The 9th Air Force had no B-25s in its combat inventory!

To the average layman of the time, a medium bomber was a medium bomber and most were familiar with the B-25 because of the Doolittle Raid on Tokyo while the few who did know what a B-26 was only knew it by the bad reputation earned in early training days that prompted calling it 'The Widowmaker' as one of its many derogatory nicknames. Tragically, the 'Widowmaker' mentality also existed to a great degree in the Air Force itself. Marauder crews in the ETO suspected that the Stateside back-burner manipulators had infiltrated *Life*'s art department and had finally brushed the Marauder off the stove top. The drawing went beyond artistic licence and was a slap in the face never to be forgotten!

At any rate, the D-Day missions flown by the 9th were the first in which they directly supported the ground forces as a true Tactical Air Force should. From then on they continued to do so and close support became routine. The shadow cast over the 9th's exploits by the 8th's propaganda mill began to shrink but the prejudices and biased actions of the strategic bombing hierarchy continued to defame the IX Bomber Command and the Marauder. Maybe they were afraid the 8th would lose its 'Mighty' monicker since the 9th was actually the largest Air Force in the world with more personnel, more aircraft (gliders included), more commands and more air bases than the 8th! Who knows!

Bombardier Charles Middleton in the 496th Bomb Squadron recalls:

At 0100 hours on the 6th I was sleeping soundly, only to be aroused by the GQ at about 0130 for the morning briefing. I haven't the slightest idea what I had for breakfast. As for clothing, I wore what I usually did to fly a combat sortie – a uniform shirt and trousers over my pyjamas and a flight suit over the uniform – plus an A-2 jacket. I wore my billed, '50-mission crush' hat because a flak helmet fitted over it. I had on my brown riding boots, which wouldn't come off if we had to bale out – and my fleece-lined flying boots, which fitted better than with the GI boot. In-flight clothing of a sort was added – a Mae West and a parachute harness. I kept my chest pack on the radio operator's table. Over all this went a flak jacket, usually donned when nearing France.

The mission briefing took place at 0230 hours. One of the main points I vividly recall was the number of German aircraft that could be brought against us, but not to worry – there would be 7,000 Allied airplanes in the air! The weather was ghastly: low clouds, drizzle and fog. As I recall, we took off about 1400 hours. The attempt to join up in proper formation was a mess. We missed the main formation and chased the group halfway across

B-26 bombing an airfield in France in May 1944. *(USAF)*

the Channel; as the sky brightened we caught up with them and took a position that looked empty. I thought then, and still do, that I was in the 13th Marauder to cross the *Utah* beachhead, regardless of mission logs, group histories and that sort of thing. The 344th had been selected to lead all the other groups, so we were the first.

Crossing the Channel, it looked to me as if you could walk ship to ship without getting your feet wet. As we neared the coast we could see naval gunfire and some return fire. We were scheduled to be over the beach before the troops came ashore, at about 0630 hours. Because of the low cloud deck, our bombing altitude was low at about 3,500 feet. We flew parallel to the shore line and dropped our 250lb bombs directly on the beach, in the sand. I thought to myself that we were digging foxholes and exploding mines. As far as we were concerned, it was a 'milk run'. The return to Stansted, three hours and fifty minutes later, was uneventful. Thus ended my thirtieth combat sortie.

Middleton went on to fly sixty-seven sorties and 230 hours of combat time before finishing his tour on 11 September 1944.

On 24 July the 344th Bomb Group dispatched thirty-nine Marauders to attack the Loire bridge near Tours in the St Lô area. On the bomb run an intense barrage of anti-aircraft fire dispersed the lead flight, but the remainder of the Group held together and despite thirty-one B-26s being damaged, attacked and destroyed vital parts of the bridge. For this mission, plus an attack on troop concentrations the following day and an attack on a supply depot during the 26th which caused great damage, the 344th Bomb Group was later awarded a Distinguished Unit Citation.

The air depot at Stansted was operated as the 2nd Tactical Air Depot with the 30th and 91st ADGs (Air Depot Groups) and was primarily concerned with the major overhaul and modification of B-26 aircraft. These activities were also eventually transferred to France and Stansted then continued in use by the USAAF as a Base Air Depot Area airfield for storing combat aircraft types that would go to the 8th Air Force bases as and when required. To facilitate storage, only the main runway was used, the others becoming parking places for lines of B-17s and P-47s. Following the end of the European War Stansted was used as a 'Rest & Rehabilitation' centre for American troops, including the famous 82nd 'All American' and 101st 'Screaming Eagle' Airborne units, on their way home to the USA. The USAAF withdrew from the depot area on 12 August 1945 and the station was taken over by the 263 Maintenance Unit RAF for storage. Between March 1946 and August 1947 one of the domestic sites at Stansted was used to house German PoWs. From December 1946 the technical facilities and relatively good accessibility to major road and rail links found the airfield used by a number of civil operators with eventual acquisition by the British Airports Authority. During the 1950s the runway had been extended to 10,000 feet by the USAF 803rd EAB as a Cold War reserve base but it was not until the 1980s that the airfield was seriously developed as London's third airport, formally opening as such in 1990.

Marauders of the 323rd Bomb Group on 13 December 1943 when 216 B-26s in four Marauder groups set out for Schiphol airport. Some 208 Marauders attacked. Eight formations of from fifteen to thirty-six aircraft each dropped 787 1,000-lb bombs, 65 per cent of them landing in the target area. The hangar and repair shop area on the south side of the field was well covered with bursts and many bombs landed on runways, taxi strips and aircraft shelters. Flak was intense and the 323rd Bomb Group lost *Raunchy Rascal* and Lieutenant George F. Pipher's crew over the target and six men wounded. Forty B-26s were hit by flak, of which three crash-landed. The *Flying Dutchman* piloted by Lieutenant Van Antwerp in the 453rd Bomb Squadron received 150 holes during the action, some 'as large as a dinner plate'. Every B-26 in the 453rd Squadron received battle damage and next day only five of the Squadron's seventeen B-26s were fit for operations. The 322nd Bomb Group put fifty B-26s over the target and lost one Marauder and thirty-four aircraft damaged by flak, plus two crash-landed on their return. The 386th Bomb Group lost *Hell's Fury* and Captain Sandford's crew from a direct flak hit and had thirty-five B-26s damaged by flak. *Man O'War* was so badly shot up that the pilot had to belly it in at Stansted depot. The 387th Bomb Group escaped loss but had thirty-eight B-26s damaged by flak. (*USAF*)

15

WETHERSFIELD
(Station 170)

Allocated to the 5th Wing in the 8th Air Force in August 1942, Wethersfield was later scheduled for loan to 3 Group RAF Bomber Command from December 1942 to May 1943. Although the main 6,000 feet and the two 4,200 feet runways with fifty loop hardstandings and one single pan in front of the butts were built, Wethersfield was not completed until the following winter by which time it had come under 9th Air Force control. Two T2 hangars and the

The three-man crews of the A-20s did sterling work in Europe, although not everyone thought the Havoc an ideal type for the theatre. The gunner in the centre of this 416th Bomb Group crew carries the single machine gun operated from the ventral position. *(USAF)*

Eight 671st Squadron A-20s over the Essex countryside. *(USAF)*

standard technical facilities were constructed on six dispersed sites to the south-west of the runways with mostly Nissen hut accommodation for 2,606 personnel.

The 416th Bomb Group (Light) equipped with Havoc solid-nose G and H versions and the J and K models with bombardier provision, was the first unit to occupy the new base, on 1 February 1944. The 416th Bomb Group, which was commanded by Colonel Harold L. Mace, was the first of three 9th Air Force light bomber groups to receive Douglas A-20 Havocs, a type on which the 416th had trained. The component squadrons of the 416th were the 668th, 669th, 670th and 671st. The Group was assigned to the 97th Combat Bomb Wing and placed on operational status on 3 March. The 416th would generally operate much like the Marauder groups by bombing from medium altitudes, those aircraft not configured to carry a bombardier flying 'in trail' with lead ships that did. To overcome any perceived drawbacks in operating solid-nosed A-20s, the light-bomber groups had to adopt formation or 'trail' bombing on bombardier signal. This resulted in a relatively small weight of bomb delivery: each A-20 carried a maximum of 2,000 lb in the internal bay, boosted, from the later-production A-20Gs onwards, by an additional 2,000 lb under the wings on four racks holding up to 500 lb each. The Group had to undergo a concentrated period of re-training in the medium-altitude formation bombing methods employed by IX Bomber Command. Despite this, it was able to fly its first mission on 4 March when twenty-one A-20s were despatched to various enemy airfields along with 251 B-26s, but solid overcast ruled out any bombing and the mission was aborted.

On 27 May the 416th and the two other Havoc groups set out to bomb the marshalling yards at Amiens. It was a disaster and when the leading 409th was forced to abort the mission, the mission lead passed to the 416th Bomb Group, which had a number of aircraft damaged by flak. The Wethersfield group was then hampered by a navigational error that put them near Poix, miles south of Amiens. As they circled around with Clermont to their left and Beauvais to their right Major M. W. Campbell, CO of the 669th Squadron and the Group lead gave the order to abandon the mission. The formation passed out over the coast

A-20G/K *Oklahoma Belle* **in the 409th or 416th Bomb Group with an unusual bomb log and Varga's 1944** *Pistol Packin Mama* **pin-up on the nose.** *(USAF)*

Colonel (later General) Harold L. Mace CO and his A-20G 43-9701 5H-H in the 668th Bomb Squadron. Mace later commanded the 98th Combat Bombardment Wing. *(USAF)*

at St-Valery-en-Caux, most of the Havocs still with their bombs aboard. That evening all three A-20 groups ventured to Amiens again. Led by three 'Window' ships, the Havocs of the 416th appeared over Amiens and were confronted by a 'wall of flak' 6,000 feet wide by 2,000 feet high. The A-20G flown by 1st Lieutenant Lucian J. Siracusa, an Australian, was hit in the right wing and the Havoc lurched out of formation, trailing smoke from a ruptured fuel tank. The bomber crashed and burned east of Bertangles. All three crew members survived and they were taken into captivity. The intense flak barrage also claimed the A-20G flown by 2nd Lieutenant Harry Earl

Hewes Junior in the 669th Bomb Squadron causing an uncontrollable engine fire. All three crew managed to bale out and they survived. A third 669th Squadron Havoc was lost when the Group pulled off the target. A burst ignited a wing tank of the A-20G flown by Allen W. Gullion Junior, who could not prevent the aircraft from making a long dive towards the ground. All three crewmen jumped out of the aircraft before it exploded in the Bois des Parisiens at Vignacourt. Short bombing by the 416th, undoubtedly due to the heavy flak, had again resulted in demolition of and damage to dwellings well clear of the rail tracks.

Colonel Mace leading the Group in A-20G 43-9701. *(USAF)*

A flight of A-20s in the 671st Bomb Squadron, 416th Bomb Group.
(USAF)

On D-Day the 416th Bomb Group flew their first mission at 1300 hours, dispatching fifty-four aircraft. The ceiling was low and the A-20s crossed over the Channel and the invasion beaches, covered with landing barges, men and equipment, at just 2,000 feet. Their target was a crossroad in the centre of Argentan. Dropping their bombs from 1,700 feet the Havocs destroyed the crossroad but bombs also hit the town. All the A-20s returned safely to base. In the afternoon of 6 June thirty-six A-20s of the 416th Group flew their second mission of the day when their target was a German strongpoint threatening the beachhead. The Havocs soon hit overcast, which separated the second box as well as three aircraft from the lead box, leaving fourteen aircraft to hit the primary target. Despite flak, the Group made its run into the objective at 12,000 feet, the briefing having stated that, if the conditions were very bad, the attack was to be made from as low as 2,000 feet! Shortly after take-off, the leader's radio had gone out and the deputy lead aircraft flown by Captain Richard K. Bills took over, his task being to guide the second box of bombers and follow the first into the target – which was fine if the first box could be seen. Bills and his aircraft headed off to try to catch up. As the Havocs crossed the Channel, the ceiling relentlessly lowered, driving the formation dangerously low as it crossed over the enemy coast at 4,000 feet. Circling once to give the other pilots a chance to re-group Bills then made his target run-in with visibility down to less than a mile. Weaving to avoid the worst of the light and heavy flak, the Havocs approached the IP. Bills' crew were pleased to see the first box of A-20s approaching the target; their navigation had been spot-on. Throwing up a vicious box barrage, the German gunners hit three A-20s immediately; committed to the bombing run, Bills waited for the

An A-20 in the 669th Bomb Squadron, 416th Bomb Group, coming off the target. *(USAF)*

A-20J 43-10129 in the 416th Bomb Group on fire after being hit by flak on the mission of 12 May 1944. *(USAF)*

bombardier to utter the magic words. When 'bombs gone!' came at last, the pilot wrenched the A-20 into a steep-diving left turn. Behind it, the flak was going wild, with hundreds of rounds bursting. Bills' turret gunner, Staff Sergeant William A. Meldrum, blazed away at the ground guns. The indifferent weather caused some of the Havocs to experience icing on the return leg. Having had his radio destroyed, Bills headed for home with another A-20 sticking close to his ship. He landed safely at Wethersfield despite a flat tyre and the A-20 stopped just in front of a steep embankment.

At 2015 hours the A-20s went out again in bad weather. Flying at 3,000 feet the Group made their entry over France at Cayeaux. A few seconds passed and then all hell broke loose. Light flak, heavy flak, tracers and small arms fire were met continuously on the route. Leading the three boxes Major Meng stuck to his course and found the target, a vital marshalling yard on the main line south-east of Dieppe. The yard was hit hard through the greatest concentration of defensive fire the Group had ever seen. One A-20 caught fire and went down over the target. Another plane stopped flying and three 'chutes were seen. Then Major M. W. Campbell was shot down. Finally the coastline came into sight and the battered formation was over the Channel. Two damaged A-20s stayed in the air just long enough to crash-land on the English coast.

On 29 June 1st Lieutenant Wayne E. Downing in the 416th Bomb Group led one element of A-20s in an attack on St-Hilaire Vitre where advancing forces were meeting stiff opposition from a firmly entrenched enemy. On the way in weather forced the formations down to 1,500 feet where they met an intense hail of light and medium flak. Downing's A-20 was hit by several shells that peeled off about one foot of covering from the leading edge of the left wing, pierced the fuel tanks in seven places and damaged the left engine. At almost the same time, the A-20 on his wing was hit and went down in flames. He continued to lead his element despite the damage and continuing heavy enemy fire and released his bombs, shattering the target. Thereupon, he returned to England alone where, due to leaking fuel, he had to make an emergency landing at Bognor Regis on the southern English coast. Coming in he found he had a flat left main tyre but managed to set the A-20 down without further damage.

By 6 August about the only bridge still standing over the Seine was that at Oissel. A number of IX Bomber Command groups had tried to blow up the bridge but had failed. At 1000 hours on 6 August the A-20s of the 416th Bomb Group took off to have a try at it but a weather front moved in and forced them to return to base. The weather cleared in the afternoon, and the 416th took off again at 1800 hours. The enemy, well knowing the importance of the bridge, had gun

A-20 5H-B 43-9182 in the 668th Bomb Squadron. *(USAF)*

emplacements extending on each side of the river for miles. Flak bracketed the flights at the beginning of the bomb run and did not stop until the Havocs were out of range. In that time of heavy and intense AA fire the 416th put its bombs right on the bridge and destroyed it, but lost three A-20s, including the one flown by Lieutenant Colonel Farmer, the Deputy Group Commander, whose flight made two passes at the bridge to make sure. Six other A-20s failed to return to base and twenty more returned with flak damage. For this mission and operations on 8 and 9 August the Group received the Distinguished Unit Citation.

In all the 416th Bomb Group flew 141 missions from Wethersfield before moving to Melun (A-55), France, on 21 September. Twenty-one A-20s were lost during operations from Wethersfield.

Wethersfield then passed to the RAF for use by the units then assigned to the First Allied Airborne Army. Stirlings of 196 and 299 Squadrons arrived in October and flew lone night sorties in support of resistance fighters in occupied countries. Deterioration of the runways at Wethersfield caused both these squadrons to move out in January 1945 while repairs were carried out. The C-47s of 316th Troop Carrier Group at RAF Cottesmore moved in on 21 March for Operation *Varsity*, returning directly to Cottesmore after the mission when they carried paratroops of the British 6th Airborne Division to a drop north of Wesel. Three of the eighty-one C-47s were shot down by flak and four others badly damaged. No other operational units were based here before the end of hostilities and Wethersfield was put on care and maintenance.

In the summer of 1952 Wethersfield was used as a base for F-84G Thunderjets of the 20th Tactical Fighter Wing, which later re-equipped with the F-84F Thunderstreak and then the F-100 Super Sabre. The main runway was extended and numerous building improvements were carried out on the technical site. With the development of Stansted airport the 20th TFW moved to Upper Heyford in 1970 to avoid any air traffic problems. While occasionally used by some USAF flying units, Wethersfield then became the home of the 'Red Horse' organisation with a mission for quick repair of airfields. In 1990, a general reduction in USAF commitments in Europe saw the airfield mothballed. The Ministry of Defence police took over the administrative and former engineering area as a training centre in 1991.

16

WORMINGFORD
(Station 159)

Construction of this Class A bomber base was undertaken by Richard
Costain Limited with additional sub-contractors during 1943. The
runways were standard, one at 6,000 feet and two 4,200 feet long and
fifty loop hardstandings were also built. The two hangars were the
usual T2 type. Eight domestic sites had utility buildings for 2,894
personnel. Originally intended for 8th Air Force use as a heavy
bomber base, Wormingford was temporarily loaned to the 9th Air
Force in late 1943 to accommodate the 362nd Fighter Group, whose
CO, Colonel Morton D. Magoffin, a fighter pilot for over five years,
and personnel arrived on the last day of November to find much
building work still underway on the technical, barrack and
communal sites. Several weeks were to pass before the full
complement of P-47 Thunderbolts arrived but enough were on hand
when the first mission, a introductory sweep over the enemy-held
coastline, went ahead on 8 February 1944. Escorts of heavy bombers
and some fighter-bomber missions were flown before the Group
moved south to Headcorn ALG on 15 April. Five P-47s were missing
in action from Wormingford and the same number of enemy aircraft
claimed in air battles.

   By this time it was clear that the base would not be required for
heavy bomber use and instead the 55th Fighter Group, 8th Air Force,
arrived and was to remain until after the end of hostilities. On 10
October 1945 Wormingford was officially transferred to the RAF
and was used during 1946 by RAF Transport Command as a base
where the camouflage paint could be removed from its aircraft,
notably Dakotas. At the end of January 1947 the airfield became a
government store. During the 1950s, Woods Ltd, an air movement
equipment manufacturer in Colchester, used the airfield for the
company's Aero Commander executive transport. The hangars and

other buildings were auctioned in 1962 and the land returned to farmers or sold. The greater part of the landing ground site was bought by the Hodge family and farmed, more land being brought into cultivation especially after 1964–65 when the St Ives Sand and Gravel Company removed hard core for the redeveloped A12 trunk road. In the late eighties, a gliding club from Suffolk regularly used Wormingford and was given planning permission to continue its activities in 1992.

Summary of Airfields and Other Locations

Andrews Field (Great Saling) (Station 485)
Description: American medium bomber base.
Location: About 4 miles west of Braintree, to the north of the A120 (the old Roman Stane Street).
Comments: Small brick pillar memorial with brass plaque records the units that served at Andrews Field.
See also, Great Saling.

Ashdon
Comments: On unclassified road 3 miles north-east of Saffron Walden. In the church is a plaque in memory of Mrs Elizabeth Everitt, a local farmer's wife, who saw an A-20 Havoc of the 409th Bomb

Andrews Field showing the ever encroaching gravel pits. *(Author)*

Group crash in a field during 1944. She attempted to rescue the crew but the blazing aircraft exploded killing them and Mrs Everitt. She is also commemorated in the tower at Little Walden, the airfield from which the A-20 took off.
See also Little Walden.

Billericay
Location: On the B1007 south of Chelmsford and east of Brentwood on the A129.
Comments: Christopher Martin, the purser and governor of the *Mayflower*, came from Billericay, a town with many weatherboard buildings similar to those in New England. Billerica in Massachusetts is no doubt connected with this town.

Birch (Station 149)
Description: American fighter base.
Location: On land near Birch Holt Farm near the village of Messing.
Comments: Much of the airfield layout is still in evidence and one group of dispersals is still in existence but almost all the buildings have disappeared.

Birch airfield in 2006. *(Author)*

Excavation during airfield construction. *(USAF)*

Boreham (Station 161)

Description: American fighter base.

Location: About 3½ miles north-north-east of Chelmsford, 2 miles north-west of the A12 at Boreham.

Comments: In July 1990 the Essex Police Air Support Unit began operating their Aerospatiale Twin Squirrel from the airfield, and in 1992 a hangar to house this helicopter was constructed beside the control tower. In 1997 the Essex Air Ambulance joined them on the airfield and a second hangar was constructed for their use in 2000. The runways and forty loop hardstands still remained in 1993 and the south-west hangar was in use as a store. Some stretches of runway remain but virtually all traces of buildings have gone.

On unclassified road off A12 at the main entrance to the former Marauder base, a stone pillar erected by the Essex Anglo-American Goodwill Association bears the EAAGA badge and is inscribed: 'We salute and commemorate the courage of our gallant allies of the American Army Air Force who flew out against the enemy from this Essex airfield 1941–45 [sic].' (The 394th Bomb Group (M) flew Marauders from Boreham between March and July 1944.) The memorial was unveiled on 5 June 1948 and a US forty-eight-star flag is displayed in nearby St Andrews Church. In 1990 a second memorial (a rough stone obelisk with bronze plaque) to the 394th Bomb Group was sited on the airfield at the instigation of the Ford Motor Co. and the Pioneer Aggregates gravel extraction company, which has workings here. This was dedicated in 1991.

Boxted (Langham) (Station 150)
Description: American fighter base.
Location: 5 miles north-east of Colchester, west of the A12 on the B1066.
Comments: Until it was stood down, the Royal Observer Corps had an underground bunker in the excavation where the fuel dump tanks had been removed. In 1990, an agricultural merchant built an office complex on the site of No. 1 hangar. In July 1992 on a remnant of the main runway at Park Lane, Langham, a brick memorial with an airfield plan and a plaque was erected to the units that served at Boxted. Very little remains of the airfield site, which has been returned to agriculture. Some of the buildings in the main technical site, including the briefing and crew rooms, both large Nissen structures, are still used for light engineering.

Braintree
Location: Town centre.
Comments: Braintree, Massachusetts, was founded in 1640 by members of the 'Braintree Company', a secret congregation of religious dissenters who chartered a ship called *The Lyon* to take them to New England, A model of *The Lyon* and a mural of the sailing can be seen in Braintree Town Hall Centre.

Victoria Street Community Centre has an American Room to remember the 20th Tactical Fighter Wing based at Wethersfield during the 1950s and 1960s. At White Court Park a memorial honours the medical achievements of the 121st and 12th US Army Hospitals. The hospital was specially prepared to take the sick and injured aircrew of the 8th and 9th Air Forces; following D-Day the majority of patients were those flown from the battlefields of Europe.

Brentwood
A thriving town close to London, there are Brentwoods in New Hampshire, Vermont and Arkansas.

Castle Hedingham
The well preserved Norman castle, which gives the village its name, was constructed by the de Vere family in 1140. The present owner is a descendant of Edmund de Vere, 17th Earl of Oxford, who has a

Heraldic glass in Chelmsford Cathedral for those who served in USAAF in Essex. *(Author)*

strong claim to have written the plays and sonnets attributed to William Shakespeare. This claim has won favour in America with the formation of the Shakespeare Oxford Society at Baltimore, Maryland.

Chelmsford city centre

At the former Marconi Head Office in Chelmsford are two plaques. One is in memory of the 397th Bomb Group which flew Marauders from Rivenhall airfield in 1944 and which was used for electronics research by Marconi. The other plaque was presented to the company by the 397th Bomb Group Association at the same time as the first, on the 40th Anniversary of D-Day, and was dedicated on 17 June 1984.

In the South Porch of the cathedral is some heraldic stained glass and in the library above, carved and coloured oak doors, oak benches with carved insignia, an inscribed floor of Portland stone and notice boards. The work is dedicated to the 'tasks and friendship shared by the people of Essex and the United States Air Force between 1942 and 1945' and was dedicated on 17 October 1953, the same day as the

Runnymede Memorial (qv). The English-Speaking Union and the Essex Anglo-American Goodwill Association, which was subsequently merged with the Union, were responsible for the scheme, which involved the rebuilding of the porch. The window as a whole commemorates those who served with the United States Army Air Forces in Essex between 1942 and 1945.

The historic connections between Chelmsford and the United States are many. The Reverend Thomas Hooker (1586–1647), a leading figure in the spiritual life of the New England settlers, was declared by President John Adams to be the author of 'the first written constitution known to history that created a government and it marked the beginning of American democracy, of which Thomas Hooker deserved more than any other man to be called the father'. Hooker was curate of the Church of St Mary (now Chelmsford Cathedral) and Town Lecturer (1626–1629). The town of Hartford, Connecticut, was founded by Hooker and his congregation. There is a Chelmsford in Massachusetts and two in Canada – in Ontario and in Northumberland County, New Brunswick. Chelmsford is also notable for the Washington family connection and their coat of arms is shown in the third light of this memorial window. This coat of arms decorated a panel of glass at Sulgrave Manor built by Lawrence Washington soon after the accession of Queen Elizabeth I. Above, in the room over this porch which houses a library donated in 1679, is another memorial window. In the centre light of the window is the emblem of the United States Army Air Forces.

Chipping Ongar (Willingale) (Station 162)
Description: American medium bomber base.
Location: 2 miles north-east of High Ongar.
Comments: Little of the airfield, except for a few buildings, remains. One of the T2 hangars was dismantled and is now in use at North Weald.

Colchester city centre
A memorial seat in the rebuilt shopping complex at Trinity Square was unveiled in 1975. It recalls the American occupancy of bases in the area.

Duxford (Station 357)
Description: RAF and American fighter base, now the IWM Duxford.
Location: East of the A505 Royston to Newmarket road off the M11.

Earls Colne, now a leisure complex. *(Author)*

Comments: The AirSpace exhibition space features twenty-five military and civil aircraft displayed both on the floor space and suspended as if flying. These rare and historic aircraft represent the story of British aviation through the twentieth century. Alongside the collection of aircraft are interactive displays about aircraft, how they fly and how they are made. The interactive displays are fun for all ages and every level of interest; AirSpace includes an area devoted to aircraft conservation, for which Duxford is world famous, where visitors can see vital conservation work taking place. The exhibition space also contains supporting displays of engines, vehicles, weapons and other items from the Imperial War Museum's collections. The 12,000 square metres of AirSpace tells the story of British aviation from the early pioneering days through to what the future may hold. The displays are a mix of video and sound, items to handle, computers, words, pictures and hands-on displays. The first floor gallery is a superb way to view all the exhibits.

Earls Colne (Station 358)
Description: American medium bomber base.
Location: On the Marks Hall estate beside the B1024 south of Earls Colne.
Comments: The wartime runways have disappeared but the perimeter

track is still in existence and is used as a service road and there are a number of wartime buildings still in use. The centre of the airfield is a golf course while an active general aviation strip occupies the northern side of the old base. This is operated by Anglia Flight Centre, which uses two runways, one of grass and one of asphalt. Off the B1024 beside the driveway into the Earls Colne Industrial Park, which occupies part of the wartime airfield, is a large brick sign listing all the businesses operating here. At the top is a side elevation of a P-51D Mustang. In the arboretum of the Marks Hall estate, where the mansion was the 9th Air Force HQ in England, is a memorial featuring a scale replica of the airfield layout and a plaque. The hall was demolished shortly after the end of the war.

Gosfield (Station 154)
Description: American fighter base.
Location: West of A1017 at Gosfield.
Comments: Little remains of the old airfield save for one stretch of runway, parts of the perimeter track and a few buildings. On the A1077 outside Maurice Rowson Hall is a Georgia grey granite boulder bearing a bronze plaque in memory of the men of the 410th Bomb Group (L) who lost their lives during World War 2. The Group operated A-20 Havocs from Gosfield between April and September 1944. The memorial, which was dedicated in May 1991 and features a head-on view of an A-20, was made in Colorado Springs and flown to England by the Transportation Squadron of the 410th Bomb Wing.

Great Dunmow (Little Easton) (Station 164)
Description: American medium bomber base.
Location: By Little Easton village on the Easton Lodge estate, north of the trunk road from Colchester to Bishop's Stortford.
Comments: On the A120 2½ miles west of town at the old Strood Hall entrance to the former USAAF Marauder base is a pillar erected by the Essex Anglo-American Goodwill Association bearing the EAAGA badge and the inscription: 'We salute and commemorate the courage of our gallant allies of the American Army Air Force who flew out against the enemy from this Essex airfield 1941–5 [sic].' The 386th Bomb Group (M) operated Marauders from Great Dunmow between September 1943 and October 1944. The memorial was refurbished by the 386th Bomb Group Airfield Research Society and in 1982 they added plaques to the east and west faces as a full roll of honour for the

386th. The Great Dunmow Museum has a collection of 386th Bomb Group memorabilia.
See also Little Easton.

Great Saling
In the village on a lawn in Vicarage Close is a brick bird-bath-style monument with plaques reading:

> The 819th Engineer Aviation Battalion of the United States Army arrived in Great Saling, Essex, in July 1942. We came as allies of the British people to construct heavy bombardment stations for the United States Eighth Air Force. The airdrome near this site was commissioned in the summer of 1943 and named Andrews Field in memory of General Frank M. Andrews of the US Air Force. It was the first airdrome constructed by American troops.
>
> The warmth and generosity of the British people in this community has not been forgotten. This marker is dedicated to these friends and to our comrades who later made the ultimate sacrifice in Western Europe, August 23 1975.

Harwich
Christopher Jones, master of the *Mayflower*, was born in the port of Harwich. His house at 21 King's Head Street is marked with a Blue Plaque.

Little Easton
Description: Little Easton Parish Church near Great Dunmow.
Location: On unclassified road off A130, 11 miles west of Braintree.
Comments: The Window of the Crusaders and the Window of Friendship and Peace in memory of the 386th Bombardment Group (M), which operated from Great Dunmow for only a year and a month (between September 1943 and October 1944), can be found in the existing organ chapel, which has been renamed the American Memorial Chapel. They were dedicated by the Bishop of Colchester on 5 October 1990.

Little Walden (Hadstock) (Station 165)
Description: American fighter base.
Location: Off the B 1052 Saffron Walden road, 13 miles north of the village and 3 miles north of Saffron Walden in what was formerly Little Walden Park.

The windows of the
Crusaders and the window of
Friendship and Peace at
Little Easton. *(Author)*

Comments: The runways have long since gone but the perimeter track remains. Some buildings in the technical area are still in use and the control tower, which was renovated for use by a local firm, has been converted into a house. There is a plaque reading:

In commemoration of the men of the 409th Bombardment Group (L) United States Army Air Force who served their country in the European conflict during World War II. Hadstock airfield station 165 was occupied by the 409th with its 640th, 641st, 642nd and 643rd Squadrons and support units from 7 March to 26 September 1944. During this period of time the Group flew 123 combat missions in the A-20 Havoc light attack bomber at Station A48 in Bretigny (Seine et Oise) France. The Group converted to the A-26 Invader light attack bomber during November 1944. The Group concluded operations on 3 May 1945 with 257 combat missions at Laon/Couvron (Aisne) France. The men of this organisation served to preserve the right of nations to determine their own destiny. Presented by the 409th Bombardment Group Association 1985.

Photographs of aircrew and Mustangs flank a plaque for the 361st Fighter Group. A second plaque reads: 'In memory of the airmen of the 361st Fighter Group US 8th Air Force who gave their lives in the defence of freedom 1943–1945'.

There is also a plaque in memory of Mrs Elizabeth Everitt, a local lady who died while attempting to rescue the crew from a crashed A-20. (*See also* Ashdon.) The operations block is now a garage.

Madingley, Cambridgeshire
Description: Cambridge American Cemetery.
Location: Approximately 3 miles west of Cambridge on the A1303.
Comments: This imposing cemetery and memorial, which covers thirty acres, was constructed on behalf of the American Battle Monuments Commission in 1956 and is dedicated to the lives of the US service personnel who perished whilst serving in the UK during World War 2. At the entrance is the Visitors' Building and a flagpole 72 feet high, the base of which is inscribed with the quotation: 'to you from failing hands we threw the torch – be yours to hold it high.' Running parallel with the A1303 are the Tablets of the Missing. A

An Engineering Battalion using a paving machine during airfield construction. (USAF)

Farm workers stop to watch a B-26 Marauder taking off on 7 September 1943. *(USAF)*

limestone wall extending 472 feet from the Visitors' Building to the Memorial Building is inscribed with the names of 5,126 United States personnel who died or went missing on active service. At the western end of the wall is the Memorial Building, which is divided into a chapel and a museum showing the progress of the war between 1942 and 1945. The 3,811 headstones in the cemetery are arranged in a fan of seven curved rows, all set within carefully maintained lawns. The cemetery is open daily from 8.00 am and 6.00 pm from April to September and 8.00 am to 5.00 pm from October to March. Limited parking is available outside the main entrance. Tel: 0954 201350.

Maldon
A riverside town dating back to the tenth century, Maldon gives its name to Malden, Massachusetts. The triangular tower of All Saints Church in Maldon is unique in England and dates from the thirteenth century. Inside the church is the 'Washington Window' presented in 1928 by the citizens of Malden, Massachusetts.

Marks Hall
See Earls Colne

Matching (Station 166)
Description: American medium bomber base.
Location: 1 mile east of Matching Green.
Comments: Only the perimeter track and a few buildings remain. On an unclassified road 4 miles east of Harlow on the east wall of the Matching Green parish church is a memorial plaque bearing the name and badge of the 391st Bomb Group and the following inscription.

> Between January and October 1944 American airmen of the 391st Bomb Group, 9th US Air Force were stationed at Matching Green. Whilst daily engaged in reducing German positions across the Channel they were received with warm hospitality, kindness, understanding and friendship in the surrounding villages. During these months the Group flew 6,000 sorties and dropped 18 million pounds of high explosives on Hitler's European Fortress, suffering the loss of 197 airmen killed, wounded and missing.
>
> The plaque is placed here by the surviving officers and men of the Group, in memory of our friends who did not come back, and in appreciation of your friendship, with the hope that Americans and Englishmen will continue to stand together in the great trials still to come for free men.

Also in existence, but with no permanent home, is a wooden shield bearing the words: 'In friendship to the village of Matching Green 391st Bomb Group (M) Association September 1981'.

Messing
Location: Near Colchester.
Comments: In the seventeenth century and earlier the Bush family farmed in Messing and members of the family also had land in the surrounding villages such as Feering. The church where the Bush

family were baptised contains material tracing the ancestors of President George Bush.

Nayland, Suffolk
Location: Off the B1087.
Comments: On the village war memorial is inscribed the name of 2nd Lieutenant Charles F. Gumm of the 354th Fighter Group USAAF. On 1 March 1944 P-51B 43-12410 of the 354th Fighter Group suffered an engine failure just after take-off from Boxted on a training flight. Gumm used what little airspeed he had to clear Nayland village but hit a tree and crashed in a water meadow beside the River Stour. To commemorate his courageous act in saving the village his name was added to the local war memorial and for some years his photograph hung in the church.

Purleigh
Laurence Washington, the great-great-grandfather of America's first president, George Washington, was vicar of Purleigh's church of All Saints from 1633 to 1643. Other Essex settlements with American connections include Dedham (the Sherman family); Copford (John Haynes, first governor of Connecticut); Springfield (William Pynchon, Massachusetts Bay Company); Great Stambridge (John Winthrop, founder of Boston and Governor of Massachusetts); Nazeing (John Eliot, social reformer).

Raydon (Station 157)
Description: American fighter base.
Location: On the B1070 Raydon-Hintlesham road, which crosses part of the old airfield east of the village
Comments: In St Mary's church on the B1070 the vestry doors bear the 8th Air Force emblem and the words: 'In remembrance of the men of the 353rd Fighter Group USA 8th Air Force who served in Raydon 1944–1945 and in remembrance of their return visit on the 25th August 1984'.

A memorial on the remains of the runway has two battered propeller blades on brick plinths with the central plinth showing a plan of the airfield, outlined in a chequer board markings of the Group, and plaque with the inscription:

> From this former airfield, during World War Two, fighter aircraft of the USAAF flew operations that contributed to the Allied Victory in Europe, 833rd Aviation Engineer Battalion,

Raydon airfield. *(Author)*

The former technical site at Raydon looking towards Gypsy Row.
(Author)

A Marauder comes into land after flying back over 100 miles on one engine in May 1944. The pilot was listed as MIA on another mission a short time later. *(USAF)*

862nd Aviation Engineer Battalion, 357th Fighter Group, 358th Fighter Group, 353rd Fighter Group and their support units. Sincerely dedicated to those so far from home who came to help us in our hour of need. 10th June 1995.

The area in front of the plinth shows the 8th Air Force badge and their history boards on either side.

Rivenhall (Station 168)
Description: American medium bomber base.
Location: North of village.
Comments: Most of the airfield structure including both the T2 hangars still exist although the north side is rapidly disappearing as the sand and gravel pit there is further enlarged.
See Chelmsford.

Saffron Walden, Essex
Description: Site of a USAAF Memorial and Wing HQ in World War 2.
Comments: The 65th Fighter Wing Memorial Apse or 'Anglo-American Memorial', as it is known, near Bridge End Gardens in the town centre, is 'In honoured memory of the officers and men of the

65th Fighter Wing of the United States Air Force and the men and women of the Borough of Saffron Walden who gave their lives in the defence of freedom 1939–1945.' It is set in a rose garden and was dedicated in 1955. The names of the casualties are listed on stone tablets for all groups in the wing.

Snailwell, Cambs (Station 361)
Description: American fighter base.
Location: Off A142, to right, just north of Newmarket.
Comments: Satellite base for Duxford, spring 1941 to December 1942, and from May to July 1944 was used by IX Air Force Service Command's Mobile Repair and Reclamation Squadrons.

Stansted Mountfitchet (Station 169)
Description: American medium bomber base, now Stansted International Airport.
Location: South-east of Stansted Mountfitchet village, east of the M11.
Comments: Virtually no trace of the wartime airfield remains although there is a group of wartime buildings used for light industry, to the west of the M11 as it passes the airport. The airport retains street names to recall the American connection with the building of the airfield in 1942 and extending it during 1954. Almost 100 USAAF units were stationed at Stansted during the period up to August 1945 and representatives of one of these, the 30th Depot Repair Squadron Association, presented the airport with a bronze memorial plaque to commemorate their stay in Essex from 17 August 1943 to 5 October 1944. The 344th Bomb Group Association also presented Stansted with a memorial plaque, and it was unveiled in the Terminal on 2 May 1992 as part of that year's reunion event.

Toppesfield, north Essex
Toppesfield is one of the many towns and villages in Essex which are associated with the early settlers of America who were driven from their homeland in order to worship freely. They took their skills and culture with them to the New World. In Topsfield, Massachusetts, named after Toppesfield, stands one of the oldest houses in New England. Built in 1683, it is weather or clap-boarded with walls of horizontal overlapping planks, a style of architecture which can be seen in many Essex towns and villages. Essex people made their marks

in commerce, government, education and in the religious life of New England from the early 1600s. In return Americans have established successful businesses here, such as the Ford Motor Company and Cossor Electronics.

Wethersfield (Station 170)
Description: American fighter base.
Location: North of the B1053 between Wethersfield and Finchingfield.
Comments: Now used by the Ministry of Defence Police as their HQ and training unit.
See also Braintree.

Wormingford (Station 159)
Description: American fighter base.
Location: 5 miles north-west of Colchester to the west of the A133 Colchester–Bures road and 1 mile south-east of the village.
Comments: A roadside memorial to the 150 casualties of the 362nd Fighter Group was dedicated in the summer of 1992 and there is a simple plaque to the 362nd over the door of what was once a guard hut.

APPENDIX 2

9th Air Force Airfields and Airstrips in the United Kingdom

Station No.	Base	A/C	Dates
485	Andrews Field	B-26	322nd Bomb Group (Medium) (12.6.43 to 25.9.44), 449th Bomb Squadron (PN), 450th Bomb Squadron (ER), 451st Bomb Squadron (SS), 452nd Bomb 1st PFS (provisional) (2.44 to 9.44) Squadron (DR) (No tail markings)
149	Birch	A-20	410th Bomb Group (Medium) (4.44)
161	Boreham	B-26	394th Bomb Group (Medium) (11.3.44 to 24.7.44), 584th Bomb Squadron (K5), 585th Bomb Squadron (4T), 586th Bomb Squadron (H9), 587th Bomb Squadron (5W), 586th Bomb Squadron (H9), 587th Bomb Squadron (5W) (White diagonal band across the fin and rudder)
150	Boxted	P-51	354th Fighter Group (13.11.43 to 17.4.44), 353rd Fighter Squadron (FT), 354th Fighter Squadron (GQ), 356th Fighter Squadron (AJ)
162	Chipping Ongar	B-26	387th Bomb Group (Medium) (1.7.43 to 21.7.44), 556th Bomb Squadron (FW), 557th Bomb Squadron (KS), 558th Bomb

Station No.	Base	A/C	Dates
358	Earls Colne	B-26	Squadron (KX), 559th Bomb Squadron (TQ) (Black and yellow diagonally marked tail band) 323rd Bomb Group (Medium) (16.10.43 to 21.7.44), 453rd Bomb Squadron (VT), 454th Bomb Squadron (RJ), 455th Bomb Squadron (YU), 456th Bomb Squadron (WT) (A broad white horizontal tail band)
154	Gosfield	P-47	365th Fighter Group (22.12.43 to 5.3.44), 386th Fighter Squadron (D5), 387th Fighter Squadron (B4), 388th Fighter Squadron (C4)
		B-26	397th Bomb Group (Medium) (4.44), 596th Bomb Squadron (X2), 597th Bomb Squadron (9F), 598th Bomb Squadron (U2), 599th Bomb Squadron (6B) (A yellow diagonal band across both sides of the vertical tailplane)
		A-20	410th Bomb Group (Medium) (16.4.44 to 27.9.44), 644th Bomb Squadron (5D), 645th Bomb Squadron (7X), 646th Bomb Squadron (8U), 647th Bomb Squadron (6Q) (An alternating black and white blocked rudder)
164	Great Dunmow	B-26 A-26	386th Bomb Group (Medium) (24.9.43 to 2.10.44) 552nd Bomb Squadron (RG), 553rd Bomb Squadron (AN), 554th Bomb Squadron (RU), 555th Bomb Squadron (YA) (A broad yellow horizontal stripe on the tail)

Station No.	Base	A/C	Dates
165	Little Walden	A-20	409th Bomb Group (Medium) (7.3.44 to 18.9.44), 640th Bomb Squadron (W5), 641st Bomb Squadron (7G), 642nd Bomb Squadron (D6), 643rd Bomb Squadron (5I) (Yellow rudder group marking)
166	Matching	B-26	391st Bomb Group (Medium) (26.1.44 to 9.44), 572nd Bomb Squadron (P2), 573rd Bomb Squadron (T6), 574th Bomb Squadron (4L), 575th Bomb Squadron (O8) (A yellow triangle on the tail fin)
157	Raydon	P-51	357th Fighter Group (30.11.43 to 31.1.44), 353rd Fighter Squadron (FT), 355th Fighter Squadron (GQ), 356th Fighter Squadron (AJ)
		P-47	358th Fighter Group (31.1.44 to 13.4.44), 365th Fighter Squadron (CH), 366th Fighter Squadron (IA), 367th Fighter Squadron (CP)
168	Rivenhall	F-5/F-6	363rd Fighter Group (1.44 to 4.44)
		B-26	397th Bomb Group (Medium) (15.4.44 to 4.8.44), 596th Bomb Squadron (X2), 597th Bomb Squadron (9F), 598th Bomb Squadron (U2), 599th Bomb Squadron (6B) (A yellow diagonal band across both sides of the vertical tailplane)
169	Stansted	B-26	344th Bomb Group (Medium) (9.2.44 to 30.9.44), 494th Bomb Squadron (K9), 495th Bomb Squadron (Y5), 496th Bomb

Station No.	Base	A/C	Dates
170	Wethersfield	A-20	Squadron (N3), 497th Bomb Squadron (7I) (White triangle on the tail fin) 416th Bomb Group (Medium) (1.2.44 to 21.9.44), 668th Bomb Squadron (5H), 669th Bomb Squadron (2A), 670th Bomb Squadron (F6), 671st Bomb Squadron (5C) (White rudder)
159	Wormingford	P-47	362nd Fighter Group (30.11.43 to 15.4.44), 377th Fighter Squadron (E4), 378th Fighter Squadron (G8), 379th Fighter Squadron (B8)

APPENDIX 3

IX Bomber Command Order of Battle – 9 June 1944

97th Combat Wing (Light)

409th Bomb Group	Little Walden	A-20
410th Bomb Group	Gosfield	A-20
416th Bomb Group	Wethersfield	A-20

98th Combat Wing (Medium)

323rd Bomb Group	Earls Colne	B-26
387th Bomb Group	Chipping Ongar	B-26
394th Bomb Group	Boreham	B-26
397th Bomb Group	Rivenhall	B-26

99th Combat Wing (Medium)

322nd Bomb Group	Andrews Field	B-26
344th Bomb Group	Stansted	B-26
386th Bomb Group	Great Dunmow	B-26
391st Bomb Group	Matching	B-26
1st Pathfinder Squadron	Andrews Field	B-26

APPENDIX 4

9th Air Force Fighter Aces (Air-to-Air Victories) ETO

Rank and Name	Group	Victories
Lieutenant William Y. Anderson	354th FG	6
Captain Don M. Beerbower	354th FG	15.5
Colonel Carl G. Bickel	354th FG	5.5
Captain Laurence E. Blumer	367th FG	6
Lieutenant Colonel Jack T. Bradley	354th FG	15
Captain Lowell K. Brueland	354th FG	12.5
Captain Bruce W. Carr	354th FG	14
Major Robert L. Coffey Junior	365th FG	6
Captain Kenneth H. Dahlberg	354th FG	14
Major James B. Dalglish	354th FG	9
Lieutenant Colonel Paul P. Douglas Junior	368th FG	7
Lt Colonel Glenn T. Eagleston	354th FG	20.5
Major Clyde B. East	10th PRG	12
Lieutenant Edward B. Edwards Junior	373rd FG	5.5
Captain Warren S. Emerson	354th FG	6
Major Wallace N. Emmer	354th FG	14
Captain Edwin O. Fisher	362nd FG	7
Major Harry E. Fisk	354th FG	5
Lieutenant Carl M. Frantz	354th FG	11
Captain Robert E. Goodnight	354th FG	7.25
Major Rockford V. Gray	365th/371st FG	6.5
Captain Joseph H. Griffin	367th FG	7
Captain Clayton K. Gross	354th FG	6
Lieutenant Charles F. Gumm Junior	354th FG	6
Major Randall W. Hendricks	368th FG	5
Captain William B. King	354th FG	5.5
Lieutenant Lenton F. Kirkland Junior	474th FG	5
Captain Charles W. Koenig	354th FG	6.5

Rank and Name	Group	Victories
Major James E. Hill	365th FG	5
Captain John H. Hoefker	10th PRG	8.5
Lieutenant Colonel James H. Howard	354th FG	8.333
Captain Edward E. Hunt	354th FG	7.5
Captain David L. King	373rd FG	5
Major George M. Lamb	354th FG	7.5
Lieutenant Leland A. Larson	10th PRG	6
Captain Charles W. Lasko	354th FG	7.5
Major Maurice G. Long	354th FG	5.5
Colonel Morton D. Magoffin	362nd FG	5
Colonel Kenneth R. Martin	354th FG	5
Captain Joseph Z. Matte	362nd FG	5
Lieutenant Donald McDowell	354th FG	8.5
Captain Joseph E. Miller Junior	474th FG	5
Lieutenant Thomas F. Miller	354th FG	5.25
Lieutenant Robert C. Milliken	474th FG	5
Captain Frank Q. O'Connor	354th FG	10.75
Lieutenant Loyd J. Overfield	354th FG	9
Lieutenant Melvyn R. Paisley	366th FG	5
Captain Robert Reynolds	354th FG	7
Lieutenant Andrew J. Ritchey	354th FG	5
Major Felix M. Rogers	354th FG	7
Lieutenant Franklin Rose Junior	354th FG	5
Lieutenant Henry S. Rudolph	354th FG	5
Lieutenant Robert L. Shoup	354th FG	5.5
Captain William J. Simmons	354th FG	6
Lieutenant Colonel Robert W. Stephens	354th FG	13
Captain Gilbert F. Talbot	354th FG	5
Lieutenant Colonel Richard E. Turner	354th FG	11
Lieutenant Robert D. Welden	354th FG	6.25

Bibliography

Arbib Robert S. Jr, *Here We Are Together, The Notebook of an American Soldier in Britain* (Privately published 1944)

Beaty, David, *Light Perpetual: Aviators' Memorial Windows* (Airlife 1995)

Blue, Alan G, *The Yoxford Boys* (Aero Publishers 1970)

Bowman Martin W., *Echoes of East Anglia* (Halsgrove Publishing Ltd 2006)

Bowman Martin W., *Great American Air Battles* (Airlife 1994)

Bowman Martin W., *USAAF Handbook 1939–1945* (Sutton 1997 2003)

Bowman Martin W., *Ghost Airfields of East Anglia* (Halsgrove Publishing Ltd 2007)

Bowyer, Michael J. F., *Action Stations 1: East Anglia* (PSL 1990)

Caldwell, Donald, *The JG 26 War Diary Vol. 2* (Grub Street, London 1998)

Condensed Analysis of the 9th Air Force in the ETO (Office of Air Force History USAF; Washington DC 1984)

Congdon, Philip *Behind the Hangar Doors* (Sonik 1985)

Cora Paul B., *Yellowjackets! The 361st Fighter Group in World War II* (Schiffer 2002)

Delve, Ken, *The Military Airfields of East Anglia Norfolk and Suffolk* (Crowood 2005)

Hale, Edwin R. W. and Turner, John Frayn, *The Yanks Are Coming* (Midas Books 1983)

Francis, Paul, *Military Airfield Architecture From Airships to the Jet Age* (PSL 1996)

Franck, Major Henry A. and 1st Lieutenant Charles O. Porter, *Winter Journey through the 9th* (Prince of the Road Press, Tucson, AZ, 2001)

Freeman, Roger A., *UK Airfields of the 9th Then and Now* (After The Battle 1978)

Hamlin, John F., *Support and Strike! A Concise History of the US 9th Air Force in Europe* (GMS 1991)

Innes, Graham Buchan, *British Airfield Buildings Expansion & Inter-War Periods* (Midland 2000)

Innes, Graham Buchan, *British Airfield Buildings of the Second World War* (Midland 1995)

Lande D. A., *From Somewhere in England* (Airlife 1991)

Marriott, Leo, *British Military Airfields Then & Now* (Ian Allan Publishing 1997)

McLachlan, Ian, *Final Flights* (PSL 1989)

McLachlan, Ian, *USAAF Fighter Stories* (Sparkford, Haynes Publishing 1997)

McLachlan, Ian, *USAAF Fighter Stories; A New Selection* (Sutton Publishing 2005)

McCrary Captain John R. 'Tex' and Scherman, David E., *First of the Many* (Robson Books 1980)

Nelson, Larry, *Historic Tales of the Wild Blue Yonder* (Privately Published 2006)

Olynyk, Frank, *Stars & Bars: A Tribute to the American Fighter Ace 1920–1973* (Grub Street 1995)

Rivenhall – the History of an Essex Airfield (Privately published 1984)

Scutts, Jerry, *B-26 Marauder units of the Eighth and 9th Air Forces* (Osprey 1997)

Scutts, Jerry, *Aces and Pilots of the US 8th/9th Air Forces* (Ian Allan 2001)

Scutts, Jerry, *US Medium Bomber Units of World War 2* (Ian Allan 2001)

Simons, Graham M., *Airfield Focus No. 81: Raydon* (GMS 2009)

Smith David J., *Britain's Aviation Memorials & Mementoes* (PSL 1992)

Spick, Mike, *Luftwaffe Fighter Aces* (Ivy Books 1996)

Stansted The War Years 1942–1945 (London Stansted Airport 50th Anniversary 1942–92)

Rust, Kenn C., *The 9th Air Force in World War II* (Aero Publishers Inc. Fallbrook, CA, 1967)

Stait, Bruce, *Bridge-Busters* (Flypast Special June 1992)

Wolf, Dr William, *Victory Roll! The American Fighter Pilots and Aircraft in WWII* (Schiffer 2001)

Young, Lieutenant Colonel Ed Barnett B. 'Skip', *The Story of the Crusaders; 386th Bomb Group in WWII* (386th Bomb Group Assn 1988)